I0018653

Lecture Notes in Information Technology

An Agent-Based Approach for Selecting and Negotiating with Suppliers in Purchasing Management

Lecture Notes in Information Technology

An Agent-Based Approach for Selecting and Negotiating with Suppliers in Purchasing Management

Meng-Jong Kuan

Yee Ming Chen

Pei-Ni Huang

Published by iConcept Press Limited

Published by iConcept Press Limited

Copyright © iConcept Press 2016

http://www.iconceptpress.com

ISBN: 978-1-922227-812

Printed in the United States of America

Contents

Preface

One consequence of market globalization has been the growing incidence of collaborative ventures among companies from different countries. Small and large, experienced and novice, companies increasingly are choosing partnerships as a way to compete in global market place. International joint ventures (IJV) have emerged as the dominant form of partnership in light of intense global competition and the need for strategic organizational viability.

Selecting a good supplier to cooperate in the supply chain is crucial to companies. It is apparent that companies have to manage in an era of global competition. Today's buyers hope cheaper price, high quality products, on-time delivery, and excellent after-sale services. And which is forcing many firms to rethink their business strategy. Achieving this starts with supplier selection. Therefore, an efficient supplier selection process needs to be in place and of paramount importance for successful supply chain management.

The main contribution of this lecture note is providing a platform architecture which can negotiate not only quantitative attributes but also qualitative attributes employed fuzzy logic. And make this negotiation mechanism is more practical in a real world and worthy to implement.

This work was financially supported by the Ministry of Science and Technology (MOST), Taiwan, R.O.C., under contract no. MOST 104-2918-I-

155-001. The authors would like to acknowledge the MOST for funding this research.

Meng-Jong Kuan
Department of Business and Entrepreneurial Management
Kainan University
Taiwan, R.O.C.

Yee Ming Chen
Department of Industrial Engineering and Management
Yuan Ze University
Taiwan, R.O.C.

Pei-Ni Huang
Graphic Design Manager
Market and Strategy Development, SINBON Electronics
Taiwan, R.O.C.

1

Introduction

1.1 Background

One consequence of market globalization has been the growing incidence of collaborative ventures among companies from different countries. Small and large, experienced and novice, companies increasingly are choosing partnerships as a way to compete in global market place. International joint ventures (IJV) have emerged as the dominant form of partnership in light of intense global competition and the need for strategic organizational viability.

Selecting a good supplier to cooperate in the supply chain is crucial to companies. It is apparent that companies have to manage in an era of global competition. Today's buyers hope cheaper price, high quality products, on-time delivery, and excellent after-sale services. And which is forcing many firms to rethink their business strategy. Achieving this starts with supplier selection. Therefore, an efficient supplier selection process needs to be in place and of paramount importance for successful supply chain management.

1.2 Problem Statement

Supplier selection begins with the realization of the need for a new supplier; determination and formulation of strategy goals, final supplier selection, the negotiating of suppliers' offer with buyer, and evaluating the performance of collaboration of suppliers and buyer. However, a successful purchasing program for buyer cannot be carried out unless cooperative buyer/supplier's relationships are maintained. So in this lecture note, we use two cases to explain different types of supply chain in suppliers selection problem, which are the manufacturer in manufacturing industry and the retailer in apparel industry. In global supply chain, there are two types governance structure to be identified: producer-driven and buyer-driven chain. And these two types will be represented into two parts in our paper.

1.3   Producer-driven vs. Buyer-driven

Traditionally, vendors are selected from among many suppliers based on their ability to meet the quantity requirements, delivery schedule, and the price limitation. In this approach, suppliers aggressively compete with each other. The relationship between buyer and supplier is usually adversarial. In this global supply chain era, the cooperation between buyer and supplier is the starting point to establish a successful supply chain management and a necessary. Therefore, supplier selection and evaluation are very important to the success of the supply chain process (Bhutta & Huq, 2002). This selection type are chosen based on producer-driven, these companies usually established international production networks to access raw materials and new overseas markets. And Chapter 2 will be described by this type of supply chain.

Beginning in the late 1960s, direct foreign investment took a new tack: it supplemented its resource-seeking and market-seeking motives for globalization with a global search for cheap labors (Gereffi, 2001). Global sourcing in buyer-driven chains is driven by intense competition among different types of developed-country retailers and marketers who feel compelled to mimic each other's moves in two ways: (a) the growth of offshore sourcing networks; and (b) utilizing brands as a source of market power (Gereffi, 2001). Global sourcing is best defined as the process of identifying, evaluating, negotiating and configuring supply across multiple geographies in order to reduce costs, maximize performance and mitigate risks. And Chapter 3 in lecture note will use apparel industry to explain this buyer-driven supply chain.

Table 1.1 summarizes two different types of supply chain alluded to above. Whereas producer-driven global value chains are characterized by vertical integration by transnational corporations based on ownership and control, and buyer-driven chains highlight the global sourcing networks established by retailers and logistic providers that rely heavily on sophisticated logistics and performance trust among numerous contractors.

Types of global supply chain	Main drivers	Form of supply chain integration	Characteristics
Producer-driven chains	Manufacturers	Vertical integration	Vertical integration with international production networks
Buyer-driven chains	Retailers logistic providers	Network integration	Global sourcing by retailers

Table 1.1 Identifications of two types of global supply chain.

1.4   Scheme for Two Parts

In Chapter 2, there are many attributes managers concerned to choose a preferred supplier, therefore, we determine suppliers' attributes by using analytic hierarchy process (AHP) in pre-selection phase. This phase is about obtaining and interpreting general information about suppliers to determine their suitability for the requirement and for working with the organization. And buyers want to focus on long-term and strategic service contracts with suppliers; those likely to be procured using model-based one-to-one negotiation approach with buyer and suppliers, so the next phase is selection procedure.

And in Chapter 3, we propose a one-to-many multi-attribute negotiation scheme which buyer/sellers agents in internet-based through negotiations have significant on supplier selection and partners' profit. And we also use Analytic Hierarchy Process (AHP) after negotiation mechanism to form a network.

1.5   Research Contributions and Structure

Our main contribution of this lecture note, based on published studies, is providing an agnent-based platform architecture (Chen & Huang, 2009) which can negotiate not only quantitative attributes but also qualitative attributes employed fuzzy logic. And make this negotiation mechanism is more practical in a real world and worthy to implement (Chen et. al., 2011).

2

Producer-driven Supply Chain: Bi-negotiation Integrated AHP in Supplier Selection

2.1 Introduction

One consequence of market globalization has been the growing incidence of collaborative ventures among companies from different countries. Small and large, experienced and novice, companies increasingly are choosing partnerships as a way to compete in global market place. International joint ventures (IJV) have emerged as the dominant form of partnership in light of intense global competition and the need for strategic organizational viability. Traditionally, vendors are selected from among many suppliers based on their ability to meet the quantity requirements, delivery schedule, and the price limitation. In this approach, suppliers aggressively compete with each other. The relationship between buyer and supplier is usually adversarial. In this global supply chain era, the cooperation between buyer and supplier is the starting point to establish a successful supply chain management and a necessary.

Therefore, supplier selection and evaluation are very important to the success of the supply chain process (Bhutta & Huq, 2002). The success of IJV depends on many factors, but the most critical include recognition of cultural differences, specified work-flow, information-sharing through electronic data interchange and the internet, and joint planning and other models that facilitate a successful supply chain management. The supplier selection negotiation mechanism is often the most complex, since it requires evaluation and decision-making under uncertainty, based on multiple attributes (criteria) of quantitative and qualitative nature, involving temporal and resource constraints, risk and commitment problems, varying tactics and strategies, domain specific knowledge and information asymmetries, etc. The negotiation cycle typically involves a sequence of interdependent activities (evaluation and decision-making) — from suppliers' selection to enter the negotiation, through the negotiation per se to the execution of the agreed deal. Supplier selection and negotiation then are of a special importance for supply chain management. Thus, the objective of this study is to develop an integrated analytic hierarchy process with negotiation mechanism which will help to solve the supplier selection problems to obtain the most beneficial offers for the buyer by creating strong competition between suppliers and providing a vehicle for negotiating with them. The rest of this chapter is organized as follows. Section 2.2 presents the methodologies of supplier selection process. The details of the methodology we proposed and the reasons that lie behind are given in section 2.3. The application is explained through a case study in section 2.4. Finally, the last section 2.5 contains some conclusions and perspectives.

2.2   Brief Review and Analysis of Supplier Selection Methodologies

1. The problem of supplier selection is not new. Before supply chain management becomes a buzzword, the problem of supplier selection was called vendor selection. First publications on vendor selection can be traced back to the early 1960s. These early research activities are summarized in a literature review by Weber *et al.* (1991). The vendor selection is also called supplier selection from now on.

2. In the literature, there are many studies about the supplier selection process. Traditional methodologies of the supplier selection process in research literature include the cost-ratio method, the categorical method, weighted-point evaluations, mathematical programming models and statistical or probabilistic approaches (Yan, Yu & Cheng, 2003; Oliveria & Lourenço, 2002). Dickson has identified 23 important criteria in the study of supplier decision-making (Dickson, 1966). A study by Vokurka looked at the supplier selection decision criteria used in buying different categories of products (Vokurka, Choobineh & Lakshmi,

1996). The myriad factors were grouped into performance criteria, economic criteria, integrative (wiliness to co-operate) criteria and adaptive criteria (the extent to which the buying firm may have to adapt its plans to accommodate uncertainty about the capability of the suppliers). The advantage of the categorical method is that it helps structure the evaluation process in a clear and systematic way. However, a disadvantage with this approach is that typically it does not clearly define the relative importance of each criterion (Muralidharan, Anantharaman & Deshmukh, 2002).

3. Weber *et al.* has compiled many articles in this area and he used a linear weighting model for supplier selection. Linear weighting models place a weight on each criterion and provide a total score for each supplier by summing up the supplier's performance on the criteria multiplied by these weights. Anukal Mandal and S.G. Desmukh used an interpretive structural modeling for vendor selection (Mandal & Deshmukh, 1994). In this study,

4. Mandal developed an analytical framework, which combines qualitative and quantitative factors. Data envelopment analysis has been used for the supplier selection process (Liu, Ding Fong & Vinod, 2000; Narasimhan, Talluri & Mendez, 2001). Another approach for supplier selection is the *analytic hierarchy approach* (Jiang & Wicks, 1999). In this study the analytic hierarchy process approach was employed to arrive at the supplier selection decision for the outsourced component of manufacturing high-end computers. It is well known that problem formulation is critical to the success of optimization.

5. Therefore, we should first answer the following questions: (1) What supplier selection criteria to use? (2) How to use them? and (3) How to automatically trade offers and come to mutually acceptable agreement? The first question is relatively easy to answer. We should use a set of criteria that are well accepted. The second question is often ignored by researchers since they usually assign fixed weights to the criteria. The last question of automating negotiations also opens up a number of new possibilities. So, we combined AHP, fuzzy set and software agents into multi-criteria decision-making and bi-negotiation mechanism. AHP deals with the traders' relative preferences and satisfactions for offers and counter-offers. In addition, fuzzy membership functions

manipulate the user's cognition for each condition and uncertainty occurring in the agents of bi-negotiation process. Meanwhile, we concentrate on the software agents for multi-issue (or "attributes") automated negotiations. This approach allows us to adapt and change the conditions for a deal dynamically. Companies rely on strategic alliances based on core competencies and information technologies to achieve flexibility and responsiveness in their supply chain (Gunasekaran & Ngai, 2005).

6. In this study, we combined AHP approach with bi-negotiation to enable the buyer and seller to cooperate to become the most competitive weapon in this market. Build-to-order supply chain can be defined as the value chain that manufactures quality products or services based on the requirements of an individual customer or a group of customers at competitive prices and within in a short span of time by leveraging the core competencies of partner firms or suppliers to integrate such a value chain. Thus, bi-negotiation let seller (supplier) know what buyer (manufacturer) wants and make a common consensus of quality products.

2.3   Methodology

A typical manufacturing company A lies in a common manufacturing supply chain, which includes its suppliers, distributors, and final customers. Company A produces the r product. It may consist of n major components, which need to be outsourced (Company A might have capacities to produce the other components by itself). For each outsourced component O_s ($s = 1,..., n$), there are k_r potential suppliers to choose from them. Each potential supplier S_p ($p = 1,..., k_r$) has a known production capacity C_p. According to the production plan, Company A will purchase q units of component from one or more suppliers out of the whole set of potential suppliers for outsourced component based on company A's predefined supplier selection criteria considering each supplier's production capacity. In summary, Company A will make decision in two phases:

a. to choose most favorable supplier(s) for various outsourced components to meet its supplier selection criteria

b. to order various quantities, prices etc. from the chosen most favorable supplier to meet its production plan.

The developed methodology for phase (a) and (b) are based on AHP approach and bi-negotiation mechanism, incorporating both quantitative and qualitative factors. To evaluate the suppliers' offers of product, we proposed a mechanism for supplier selection. The first phase was to apply decomposition-synlecture note approach using AHP approach. At the second phase, we first used linear programming to calculate buyer's offer (i.e. company A) and then used the agents of buyer and chosen supplier to automatically negotiate several times. As a result, buyer and chosen supplier can get the final satisfying offers. Steps of the algorithm based on AHP and bi-negotiation agents are briefly summarized as follows.

2.3.1   Phase A: Apply Decomposition-synlecture Note Approach using AHP

Step A1. Decomposet problem

The underlying multi-criteria decision-making problem is decomposed according to its selection issue. The overall goal of supplier selection is to achieve overall efficiency of suppliers. The efficiency measure consists of four top-level attributes, namely, assets, business criteria, cost, and delivery. Each attribute consists of a number of specific performance metrics, which are identified in next step. These attributes were determined by reviewing the literature and using a brainstorming tool with the members of the supplier chain department (Barborosoglu & Yazgac, 1997; Braglia & Petroni, 2000; Masella & Rangone, 2000; Tam & Tummala, 2001).

Step A2. Define attributes for supplier selection

Supply Chain Council (SCC) constructed a descriptive framework called SCOR (SCC, 1999). SCOR is a standard supply chain process reference model designed to embrace all industries. SCOR performance metrics are used as the second-level attributes for supplier selection. The SCOR endorses 16 performance metrics, which fall into four defining top level attributes:

a. Assets:

- Cash-to-cash cycle time (a_1) ,
- Inventory days of supply (a_2),
- Order quantity (a_3),
- Visitation to supplier facilities (a_4).

b. Business criteria

- Performance history (b_1),
- Production flexibility (b_2),
- Quality performance (b_3).
- Position in the industry and reputation (b_4),
- EDI capability (b_5),
- Organization structure (b_6).

c. Cost

- Price (c_1),
- Logistics cost (c_2),
- Value-added productivity (c_3).

d. Delivery

- Supply chain response time (d_1),
- Delivery lead time (d_2),
- Fill rate (d_3).

These performance metrics are adopted here as the standard attributes for evaluating a supplier's performance.

Step A3. Design the hierarchy

The hierarchy consists of the overall goal, top-level attributes, second-level attributes (performance metrics), sub-level (could have several levels), and the decision alternatives. Figure 2.1 schematically illustrates the proposed hierarchy based on SCOR metrics.

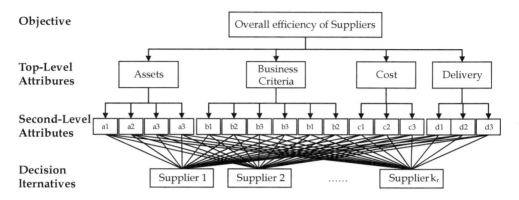

Figure 2.1: AHP hierarchy for suppliers' selection.

Step A4. Construct pair-wise comparison matrix

Once the problem has been decomposed and the hierarchy constructed, prioritization procedure starts to determine the relative importance of the elements within each level. Based on product characteristics and corresponding supply chain strategies, the relative importance of the top-level attributes and the second-level attributes (performance metrics) is determined by experienced managers.

Company *A* identifies its preference to decide the linguistic value of each attribute (Figure 2.2) to describe how much more important the *i*th attribute is than the *j*th attribute. Suppliers also were asked to indicate their preference level as to to each attribute and then to construct a comparison matrix for each attribute.

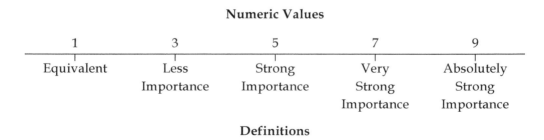

Figure 2.2: Linguistic representative preference and their numeric values.

The comparison matrix of company A for product r determining outsourced component O_s is shown in formula (1) by linguistic attribute values, $a_{ij} \in [1,3,5,7,9]$. a_{ij} represents how much more important the ith attribute is than the jth attribute.

$$O_s = \left[a_{ij} \right]_{m \times m} = \begin{bmatrix} a_{11} & a_{12} & \cdots & a_{1m} \\ a_{21} & \ddots & & a_{2m} \\ \vdots & & \ddots & \\ a_{m1} & \cdots & \cdots & a_{mm} \end{bmatrix} ,$$

(1)

$$a_{ij} = \begin{cases} 1 \ , \ i = j \\ 3,5,7,9 \ , \ \text{otherwise} \end{cases} , \ a_{ji} = \frac{1}{a_{ij}} ,$$

where i, j represents each attribute, and m represents the number of attributes.

Step A5. Normalized the comparison matrix

This step was to normalize each element of the comparison matrix in the formula (1). Each element in column i is divided by the sum of the element in column i and form a new matrix N_O_s. The sum of the element in column i of N_O_s is 1.

$$N\_O_s = \begin{bmatrix} \dfrac{a_{11}}{\sum\limits_{i=1}^{m} a_{i1}} & \dfrac{a_{12}}{\sum\limits_{i=1}^{m} a_{i2}} & \cdots & \dfrac{a_{1m}}{\sum\limits_{i=1}^{m} a_{im}} \\ \vdots & & \ddots & \vdots \\ \dfrac{a_{m1}}{\sum\limits_{i=1}^{m} a_{i1}} & \cdots & & \dfrac{a_{mm}}{\sum\limits_{i=1}^{m} a_{im}} \end{bmatrix} .$$

(2)

Step A6. Selection of optimal supplier by overall weights

We first calculated the average vector C which is the average of each element in row i of N_O_s. c_i represents the relative degree of importance for the ith attribute and evaluating score of attributes.

$$C = [c_i] = \begin{bmatrix} \dfrac{\dfrac{a_{11}}{\sum\limits_{i=1}^{m} a_{i1}} + \dfrac{a_{12}}{\sum\limits_{i=1}^{m} a_{i2}} + \cdots + \dfrac{a_{1m}}{\sum\limits_{i=1}^{m} a_{im}}}{m} \\ \vdots \\ \dfrac{\dfrac{a_{11}}{\sum\limits_{i=1}^{m} a_{i1}} + \dfrac{a_{12}}{\sum\limits_{i=1}^{m} a_{i2}} + \cdots + \dfrac{a_{1m}}{\sum\limits_{i=1}^{m} a_{im}}}{m} \end{bmatrix}. \tag{3}$$

Then using $N\_O_s \cdot C$ to form the overall weight X.

$$N\_O_s \cdot C = X = \begin{bmatrix} x_1 \\ x_2 \\ \vdots \\ x_m \end{bmatrix}. \tag{4}$$

Step A7. Consistency check

After step A_5 and A_6, we needed to check consistency in the comparison matrix. In AHP, consistency index (CI) and consistency ratio (CR) are two indexes used to test consistency of the matrix.

$$r = \frac{1}{m} \sum_{i=1}^{m} \frac{x_i}{c_i}, \tag{5}$$

$$CI \text{ (Consistency Index)} = \frac{r-m}{m-1}. \tag{6}$$

By test, assume that CI=0 represents the judgments before and after being determined by the decision maker are completely consistent. CI>0 represents the judgments are not consistent. And CI ≤ 0 represents tolerable deviation. So that means the smaller the CI value is, the higher the consistency is.

$$CR \text{ (Consistency Ratio)} = \frac{CI}{RI \text{ (Random Index)}} \tag{7}$$

CI by random is called random index (RI). And CI/RI is called the consistency ratio (CR). If CR ≤ 0.1, the degree of consistency is satisfactory, but if CR > 0.1, serious inconsistencies may exist, and the AHP may not yield meaningful results. Then we must go back to consider another more significant attribute (Kim & Selim, 2003).

2.3.2   Phase B: Bi-negotiation between Company and The Chosen Most Favorable Supplier

Step B1. Fuzzy membership function

The interaction of bi-negotiation agents happen on two levels: the first level interaction within user and software agent framework and the second between two agents. The first level of interaction involves user and software agent communicating in order to come to an agreement on what decision to take as a negotiation agent. A natural way to cope with such uncertain communication is to express the interaction as a fuzzy membership function, which incorporates the vagueness of user thinking. The second level of interaction involves bi-negotiation agents interact using offer/counter-offer to reach an agreement. At the first level, the buyer used his own preference to determine what the satisfactory degrees of each attribute are. This model assumes that each attribute had its range that can be changed by the buyer. The buyer can grade from 0 to 1 in accordance with his satisfaction degree. A triangular fuzzy membership function (Figure 2.3) with center b can be interpreted as showing attribute quantity "x is approximately in the point b". The others such as a trapezoidal fuzzy number may be seen as an attribute quantity "x is approximately in the interval". In order to better facilitate interaction between the user and software agent from a practical viewpoint, we then employed triangular membership function to determine the user linguistic value of each attribute. When the fuzzy membership function of each attribute is decided, we can then convert these human linguistic values of attributes into fuzzy value (FV). The average of fuzzy value of all attributes represents buyer's and seller's satisfaction degrees (SD).

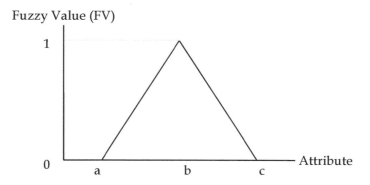

Figure 2.3: Triangular membership function.

Step B2. Determine initial offers of buyer

In *Phase A*, we already knew the offers of chosen supplier. Because the buyer wanted the average satisfaction degree to be higher, we next used *linear programming* to calculate a hypothetical counter-offer from the seller based on seller's initial requirements. Table 2.1 shows some notations about the definitions. We assumed the satisfaction degree (SD) is the average of all attributes' fuzzy values.

$$SD_B = \text{average (sum of all } FV_B) \qquad (8)$$
$$SD_S = \text{average (sum of all } FV_S) \qquad (9)$$

Notation	
IO_B	Initial offers of Buyer
IO_S	Initial offers of Seller
FV_B	Fuzzy value of Buyer
FV_S	Fuzzy value of Seller
SD_B	Satisfaction degree of Buyer
SD_S	Satisfaction degree of Seller

Table 2.1: Notation.

Step B3. Determine negotiation bargain strategy of buyer and seller

Having already determined the most suitable supplier, the buyer still hoped that the satisfaction level could be improved. So the offers between the chosen supplier and the buyer now needed to be negotiated again. For this step, a bi-negotiation mechanism using agent-based bargain strategies was used to let both sides make concessions on each attribute.

The bargain strategies were decided by the buyer and seller. The objective of bargain strategy was to find out mutually satisfying compromise between buyer and seller (In this study, the terms "seller/buyer" and "supplier/Company A" are used interchangeably).

Figure 2.4 shows bargain strategy of each condition. (a), (b), and (c) are seller's strategies and (d), (e), and (f) represent buyer's strategies. The x-axis stands for the series of negotiation offers and counter-offers, and y-axis is the changing value of each attribute from the initial offer/counteroffer represented by IO_S (seller agent) and IO_B (buyer agent).

a. The seller makes an initial offer, and then compromises. The seller then adds compromise to a larger degree as negotiations continue.

b. The seller presents an initial offer and negotiates with a series of incrementally decreasing offers.

c. The seller tries advantages an initial offer then they compromise substantially in order to let the buyer know their sincerity but stick at this lower offer.

d. The buyer tries advantages an initial offer then they compromise substantially in order to let the seller know their sincerity but stick at this lower offer.

e. The buyer presents an initial offer and negotiates with a series of incrementally decreasing offers.

f. The buyer makes an initial offer, and then compromises. The buyer then adds compromise to a larger degree as negotiations continue.

As represented in Figure 2.4, buyer and seller predetermine their patterns of compromise and these strategies can be inputted into their agents so that the negotiation process itself can be automated via the action of the agents.

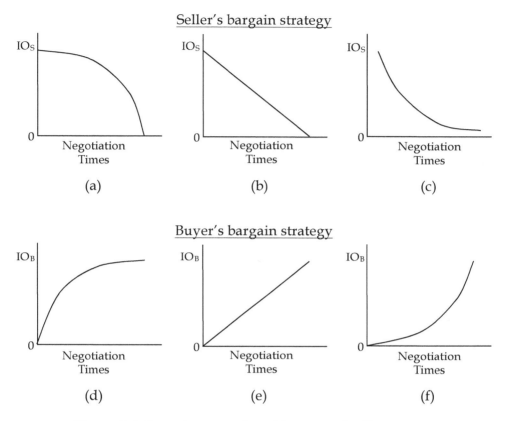

Figure 2.4: Bargain strategies of buyer and seller agents.

Step B4. Bi-negotiation process

According to step B_2 in this phase, when the initial offers of both sides were determined, we chose the biggest difference of attributes m_i between buyer and seller as our main factor to negotiate first. Then using the bargain strategies of the buyer and seller, the buyer and seller agents began to negotiate the values of each attribute. This continues until the buyer and seller agents were achieved a common consensus for all attributes at which point the negotiation stops with a mutually satisfactory offer for both sides. Figure 2.5 shows the integrated AHP with Bi-negotiation algorithm for supplier selection and negotiation process.

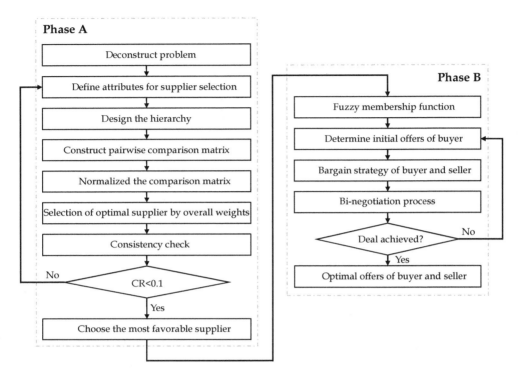

Figure 2.5 An integrated AHP with Bi-negotiation algorithm.

2.4   Case Implementation

To demonstrate this proposed mechanism for supplier selection, we used a build-to-order (BTO) computer manufacturer as our sample case. In order to maintain the confidentiality of the firm utilized in the case illustration, the high-end computer manufacturing company is referred to as Company A. It produces various functional components, such as mother boards, interface cards, and peripheral components connectivity hardware etc. The specific component to be outsourced in our hypothetical sample was the power supply unit.

It is assumed that only three potential sellers are qualified to supply the outsourced component. So, in this study three international suppliers of Company A will be evaluated and named as supplier 1 (Taiwan), supplier 2 (China), and supplier 3 (Malaysia). Supplier 1 is a famous outsourcing firm which is good at ODM. Supplier 2 emphasizes quality and makes the best products. And Supplier 3 is well-known for its production rate.

With this basic background about the suppliers, we started our supplier selection mechanism process step by step.

In *Phase A*, we create the comparison matrix of priorities attributes desired by Company *A* and each supplier relative ability to meet these requirements. To begin *Phase A*, we met with Company *A* to determine which attribute was most important to them in choosing suppliers. We arrived at four top-level quantitative and qualitative attributes which were assets, business criteria, cost, and delivery. These four were subdivide further into 16 performance metrics with respective to top level attributes. In this sample case, there were three suppliers to choose from, and we used four top-level attributes and 16 performance metrics to compare the offers of each supplier. In Table 2.2, the suppliers' information in relation to these criteria is listed for the outsourced power supply.

At this point in *Phase A*, managers of Company A were asked to prioritize the four attributes in view of the suppliers' offer to generate the accompanies matrix. This is done by using pair-wise comparison with Saaty's 1–9 scales (Figure 2.2). To compute each supplier's weights, one need is to calculate the overall priority. Overall priority is calculated by multiplying the respective terms in priority of *the top-level* by the priority of *the second-level* and *the priority of decision alternatives*. And Table 2.3~2.8 shows the process of constructing the pair-wise comparison matrices and their normalized process with the second-level attributes "Order quantity" in the top level attribute "Assets" as an example, and the same steps used to compute the other attributes. To facilitate *Phase A* calculation, Matlab® programming utilities were used.

After repeating this calculation for each of the 16 second-level attributes, all of the overall weights were computed (Table 2.9). Several implications for company manager are evident in Table 2.9. For example, "Price" (c_1), as expected, played a key role in the supplier selection process (indicated by the overall weight of 0.18169). In buying and selling situations, price is typically the most important concern for buyers. Next important to the company was "Quality performance" (b_3) (the overall weight of 0.14635). Therefore, suppliers emphasizing strong quality control would be more successful in this competition. Additionally, Table 2.9 reveals that "Supply chain response time" (d_1) and "Position in the industry and reputation" (b_4) were also important factors in supplier selection. So, the managers of suppliers can refer to this information sharing in Table 2.9 as a guide to what to prioritize in managing a company.

Attributes	Items	Sellers		
		Supplier 1	Supplier 2	Supplier 3
Assets	Cash-to-cash cycle time (a_1) / days	5	7	8
	Inventory days of supply (a_2) / days	15	11	16
	Order quantity (a_3) / units	400	380	375
	Visitation to supplier facilities (a_4) / %	90%	93%	95%
Business Criteria	Performance history (b_1) / %	85%	88%	80%
	Production flexibility (b_2) / %	78%	85%	75%
	Quality performance (b_3) / grades	5	2	4
	Position in the industry and reputation (b_4) / grades	4	3	1
	EDI capability (b_5) / %	4	3	5
	Organization structure (b_6) / grades	3	2	1
Cost	Price (c_1) / $	13	12	10
	Logistics cost (c_2) / $	30	32	40
	Value-added productivity (c_3) / grades	4	5	3
Delivery	Supply chain response time (d_1) / days	7	3	4
	Delivery lead time (d_2) / days	22	28	25
	Fill rate (d_3) / %	95%	96%	92%

Table 2.2: The initial offers of each attribute between three suppliers.

$$O_s = \begin{array}{|c|c|c|c|c|} \hline & \textbf{Assets} & \textbf{Business Criteria} & \textbf{Cost} & \textbf{Delivery} \\ \hline \end{array}$$

	Assets	Business Criteria	Cost	Delivery
Assets	1	1/3	1/5	1/3
Business Criteria	3	1	2	2
Cost	5	1/2	1	3
Delivery	3	1/2	1/3	1

Table 2.3: Initial comparison matrix of top- level attributes among the suppliers.

$O_A =$

	a1	a2	a3	a4
a1	1	2	5	3
a2	1/2	1	5	3
a3	1/5	1/5	1	1/3
a4	1/3	1/3	3	1

Table 2.4: Initial comparison matrix of second-level attributes. "Order quantity" in the top-level attribute "Assets".

$O_{a3} =$

	Supplier 1	Supplier 2	Supplier 3
Supplier 1	1	2	3
Supplier 2	1/2	1	2
Supplier 3	1/3	1/2	1

Table 2.5: Initial comparison matrix the attribute. "Order quantity" among the suppliers.

	Assets	Business Criteria	Cost	Delivery
Assets	1	1/3	1/5	1/3
Business Criteria	3	1	2	2
Cost	5	1/2	1	3
Delivery	3	½	1/3	1

$O_s =$

↓ Normalized

	Assets	Business Criteria	Cost	Delivery
Assets	0.08333	0.14286	0.05660	0.05263
Business Criteria	0.25000	0.42857	0.56604	0.31579
Cost	0.41667	0.21429	0.28302	0.47368
Delivery	0.25000	0.21429	0.09434	0.15789

$O_s =$

Table 2.6: Normalized comparison matrix of each attribute among the suppliers.

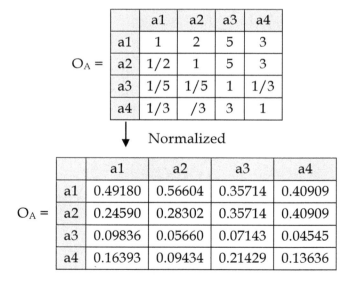

	a1	a2	a3	a4
a1	1	2	5	3
a2	1/2	1	5	3
a3	1/5	1/5	1	1/3
a4	1/3	/3	3	1

$O_A =$

↓ Normalized

	a1	a2	a3	a4
a1	0.49180	0.56604	0.35714	0.40909
a2	0.24590	0.28302	0.35714	0.40909
a3	0.09836	0.05660	0.07143	0.04545
a4	0.16393	0.09434	0.21429	0.13636

$O_A =$

Table 2.7: Normalized comparison matrix of the second-level attribute "Order quantity" in attribute "Assets".

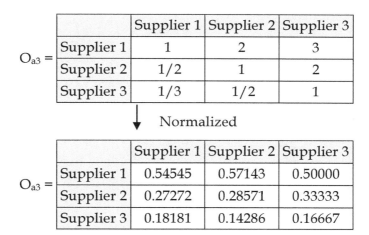

Table 2.8: Normalized comparison matrix the attribute "Order quantity" among the suppliers.

Top Level Attributes	AHP weights (C_i)	Second Level Attributes	AHP weights (Ca_i)	C.R. value	Decision Alternatives	AHP weights (Cs_i)
Assets	0.08386	Cash-to-cash cycle time (a_1)	0.03824	-1.7844	Supplier 1	0.02384
					Supplier 2	0.00526
					Supplier 3	0.00914
		Inventory days of supply (a_2)	0.02715	-1.9152	Supplier 1	0.00455
					Supplier 2	0.02004
					Supplier 3	0.00256
		Order quantity (a_3)	0.00570	-1.9195	Supplier 1	0.00307
					Supplier 2	0.00169
					Supplier 3	0.00093
		Visitation to supplier facilities (a_4)	0.01277	-1.8234	Supplier 1	0.00220
					Supplier 2	0.00669
					Supplier 3	0.00388

Continued on next page…

... Continued from previous page

					Supplier 1	0.00857
Business Criteria	0.39010	Performance history (b₁)	0.03584	-1.7844	Supplier 2	0.02235
					Supplier 3	0.00493
		Production flexibility (b₂)	0.08030	-1.9213	Supplier 1	0.01846
					Supplier 2	0.05203
					Supplier 3	0.00981
		Quality performance (b₃)	0.14635	-1.9004	Supplier 1	0.08136
					Supplier 2	0.01322
					Supplier 3	0.05177
		Position in the industry and reputation (b₄)	0.08197	-1.9168	Supplier 1	0.04842
					Supplier 2	0.02736
					Supplier 3	0.00619
		EDI capability (b₅)	0.02782	-1.8949	Supplier 1	0.00507
					Supplier 2	0.00320
					Supplier 3	0.01955
		Organization structure (b₆)	0.01782	-1.9005	Supplier 1	0.01049
					Supplier 2	0.00449
					Supplier 3	0.00284
Cost	0.34691	Price (c₁)	0.18169	-1.9053	Supplier 1	0.01929
					Supplier 2	0.04733
					Supplier 3	0.11506
		Logistics cost (c₂)	0.10553	-1.9215	Supplier 1	0.06134
					Supplier 2	0.03262
					Supplier 3	0.01157
		Value-added productivity (c₃)	0.05971	-1.9053	Supplier 1	0.01555
					Supplier 2	0.03782
					Supplier 3	0.00634
Delivery	0.17913	Supply chain response time (d₁)	0.11345	-1.8455	Supplier 1	0.07266
					Supplier 2	0.02336
					Supplier 3	0.01743
		Delivery lead time (d₂)	0.04666	-1.9161	Supplier 1	0.03428
					Supplier 2	0.00396
					Supplier 3	0.00843
		Fill rate (d₃)	0.019012	-1.8527	Supplier 1	0.00402
					Supplier 2	0.00194
					Supplier 3	0.01305

Table 2.9: All of the overall rating weights in Phase A.

The last step in the selection process is to calculate the final rank of potential suppliers for the outsourced component by using the formula (10) based on Table 2.9. The supplier selection results are shown in Table 2.10.

Based on the results for overall weights in Phase A, we recommended Supplier 1 as the most favorable supplier for the Company A. Therefore, the buyer would select Supplier 1 as their partner. Then, Company A and supplier 1 will negotiate with each other in the next phase.

$$\begin{aligned}
\text{Total weights of Supplier } i \; (TW_i) = \;& C_A \cdot C_{a_1} \cdot C_{s_i} \\
& + C_A \cdot C_{a_2} \cdot C_{s_i} \\
& + C_A \cdot C_{a_3} \cdot C_{s_i} \\
& + \cdots \\
& + C_C \cdot C_{c_2} \cdot C_{s_i} \\
& + C_C \cdot C_{c_3} \cdot C_{s_i}
\end{aligned} \qquad (10)$$

Final Rank	
Supplier 1	0.41316
Supplier 2	0.30335
Supplier 3	0.28349

Table 2.10 Supplier selection results.

2.4.1   Phase B: Bi-negotiation Between Company and The Chosen Most Favorable Supplier

Step B1. Fuzzy membership function

In this phase, the buyer and seller agents offer their negotiating positions reflecting their relative priorities for a deal. Negotiating the deal involves quantitative and qualitative attributes. Each attribute has a predetermined acceptable range for the buyer and seller. The buyer agents generate a starting value for each attribute and form within this range as the first negotiation position (Table 2.11). They then proceed to use alternate fuzzy value in response to on another's counter-offers until equitable deal is reached.

The workload involved in this process of negotiation and recalculation would be heavy if all possible combinations needed to be tried. However, this is rarely necessary because in practical negotiations, only specified attributes are negotiated and these are negotiated within a limited range of mutually desirable values (Steel & Beasor, 1999). In this negotiation, the important issues are quantity, price, quality and delivery. Figure 2.6 shows results of the fuzzy membership functions for each attribute.

Attributes	Acceptable range
Quantity	300~800 (units)
Price	10~20 ($)
Quality	1~5 (grades)
Delivery	20~30 (days)

Table 2.11: Acceptable ranges of each attribute.

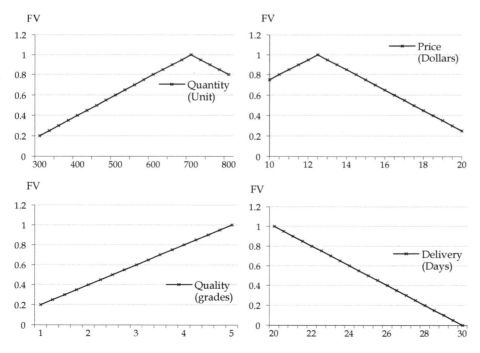

Figure 2.6: Fuzzy membership functions for each attribute from user interaction.

Step B2. Determine initial offers of buyer

After Supplier 1 was chosen, the initial offers still needed to be fine-tuned between Supplier 1 and Company A. In order to manufacture high-quality end product, Company A would like to improve the satisfaction in the supplier's offer from 78.75% to 95%. So in this step, we used linear programming to achieve this objective (Table 2.12). In Table 2.13, we can see that the fuzzy value for the attribute "Quality" between both seller and buyer was 1 which means this component's quality was assured to be high. Therefore we didn't need to negotiate this item. However, the difference between the respective fuzzy values for the attribute "Quantity" (0.4 and 1) was the greatest so we regarded this attribute as our main factor to negotiate.

Objective	$SD_B = 0.95$
Constraint	$FV_B \geq FV_S$
	$FV_B \leq 1$

Table 2.12: The objective and the constraints of linear programming.

Seller (Supplier 1)			Buyer (Company A)		
	IO_S	FV_S		IO_B	FV_B
Quantity	400	0.4	Quantity	600	0.8
Price	13	0.95	Price	12	1
Quality	5	1	Quality	5	1
Delivery	22	0.8	Delivery	20	1
SD_S		78.75%	SD_B		95%

Table 2.13: The initial offers of the seller and the buyer.

StepB3. Determine negotiation bargain strategy of buyer and seller

In this step, we first set the bargain strategy of seller and buyer then we set the agents for each side to negotiate. Figure 2.7 presents the strategy of seller agent for "Quantity". We can see that the seller will increase the quantity value steeply in the first two rounds. After that, the seller compromises less and less. The buyer agent bargain strategy as shown in Figure 2.8. The buyer will decrease the quantity value only slightly in the first five rounds. After that, the buyer decreases the quantity value to a larger degree to reach an agreement.

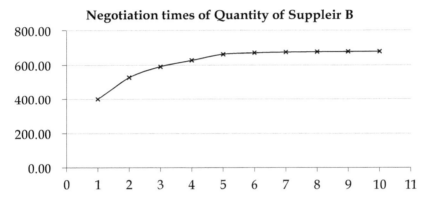

Figure 2.7: Bargain strategy of seller agent.

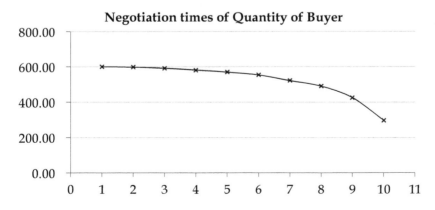

Figure 2.8: Bargain strategy of buyer agent.

Step B4. Bi-negotiation process

With the respective bargain strategies now set, the buyer and seller's agents negotiate automatically on behalf of each side to achieve common consensus with the highest possible level of satisfaction for both.

In Table 2.13, we saw that the attribute "Quantity" marked the largest gap between the needs of Company *A* and the supplier's offer. The initial offers of Supplier 1 only provided for 400 units, but the manufacturer wanted 600 units. Thus, this is where their agents began the automatic bi-negotiate process.

Figure 2.9 illustrates the bi-negotiation results each time. As we see in the figure, at the third negotiation, buyer and seller reach a common consensus for each attribute. With the exception of "Quality", all attributes adjusted their values during this negotiation. The negotiations continued until a mutually satisfactory compromise value was reached for Quality, Price, and Delivery at which point the negotiation process ended. The final offers of both sides are shown in Table 2.14. As a result of the bi-negotiation the satisfaction level approaching the target of 95%, reaching 90.8%, an increasing of 12.05% over the starting level of 78.75%.

From the moment, the supplier was chosen as the partner of Company *A*, the interaction between both sides was crucial. Integrated AHP with bi-negotiation agents provided a vehicle to negotiate and achieve a win-win situation.

2.5   Brief Summary

Supplier selection and evaluation is very important to the success of a manufacturing firm. This is because of the cost and quality of goods and services sold is directly related to the cost and quality of goods and services purchased. Therefore, purchasing and supplier selection play an important role in supply chain management. Sellers and buyers in internet-based supply chain through negotiations have significant impact on supplier selection and partners' profit. In this study, the integrated analytic hierarchical process approach with bi-negotiation agents have been proposed as a potential tool for analyzing and evaluating suppliers in the electronic supply chain. Using the main and sub-attributes for supplier selection in AHP were clearly identified and the problem solved was structured

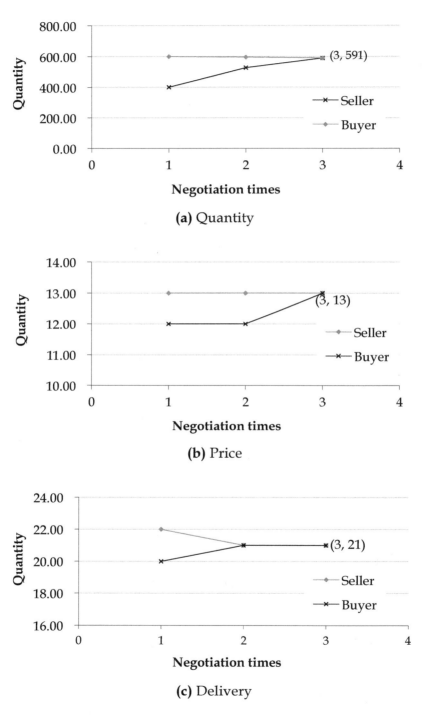

(a) Quantity

(b) Price

(c) Delivery

Figure 2.9: Bi-negotiation agents' process.

Final offers		
quantity	591	0.782
price	13	0.95
quality	5	1
delivery	21	0.9
SD		90.8%

Table 2.14: The final result between buyer and seller.

systematically. This enables decision-makers to examine the strengths and weaknesses of vendor systems by comparing them with respect to appropriate top and second-level attributes. During the decision-making between buyer and seller, it is crucial to negotiate on multiple attributes for a deal such as price, quantity, quality, delivery, and relative preferences. Therefore, this study is also attempt to develop how to elicit the user's bargain strategies in order for his autonomous agent to negotiate on their behalf. Moreover, the approach is recognized as one of the best bargain strategies for automated negotiation. Based on this work, our future extension is to investigate other decision phases in supplier selection and provide similar approaches to enrich the available literature. We will evaluate a more detailed form, the influence of other methodologies on the final quality and accuracy of decisions. We will also try to enhance our decision support system with software agents' techniques to enable managers comparing different solutions and making more rigorous and practical decisions.

3

Buyer-driven Supply Chain: Coping with Multi-Attribute Bilateral Negotiation and AHP on Supply Chain Integration in Apparel Industry

3.1 Introduction

3.1.1 Background of the Apparel Industry

With the driving forces of outsourcing and globalization, apparel supply chains have been rapidly dynamic. Product designers, marketers, and manufacturers are no longer in the same organization. More likely, they are spread over several continents in organizations with different cultures, languages, and business objectives. Branded specialty retail and contract suppliers that bring their products to market orchestrate a long supply chain starting with fibers (wool, cotton, synthetic) that are spun, woven, knit, cut and sew assembly operations. Like all products, once designed, garments are subject to many design changes in the production phases. And often changes made by brand designers are slow to reach the production floor of contract suppliers. In many companies, the change process is conducted through faxes, phone, and emails – all poor means of managing a distributed, complex supply chain. It found that transferring the information within the rapidly disintegrating supply chain was tedious. Winners in this apparel industry must find new ways to leverage their supply chain partnerships through information integration and collaboration – improving products, driving down cycle times, and reducing supply chain costs. With the opportunities of moving design processes onto the Web, apparel supply chains are currently undergoing a dramatic transformation from a producer-driven supply chain to a buyer-driven supply chain. In this buyer-driven supply chain, the third party logistic provider's ability to respond quickly to retail of branded specialty designer depends heavily upon how well it controls its supply chain, collaborates with suppliers, and manages its merchandise. Retailers have to quickly introduce new design and its changes to maintain high sales and out-pace the competition.

Global sourcing in buyer-driven chains is driven by intense competition among different types of developed-country retailers and marketers who feel compelled to mimic each other's moves in two ways: (a) the growth of offshore sourcing networks; and (b) utilizing brands as a source of market power (Gereffi, 2001). Global sourcing is best defined as the process of identifying, evaluating, negotiating and configuring supply across multiple geographies in order to reduce costs, maximize performance and mitigate risks.

Apparel is an ideal industry for examining the dynamics of buyer-driven supply chain. The relative ease of setting up clothing companies, coupled with the prevalence of developed-country protectionism in this sector, has led to an unparalleled diversity of garment exporters in the third world. Furthermore, the backward and forward linkages are extensive, and help to account for the large number of jobs associated with the industry.

3.1.2   Research Aims

Involving in global sourcing, negotiation of products' new design introduce and change issues among the third party logistic provider, branded specialty retail and contract suppliers are becoming an important process to proceed. The negotiation mechanism is often the most complex, since it requires to solve uncertainties based on multiple attributes of quantitative and qualitative nature, involving temporal and resource constraints, risk and commitment problems, varying tactics and strategies, domain specific knowledge and information asymmetries, etc. The negotiation cycle typically involves a sequence of interdependent activities—from contract suppliers' selection to enter the negotiation, through the negotiation per se to the execution of the agreed deal. Contract supplier selection and negotiation then are of a special importance for buyer-driven supply network. Thus, the objective of this study is to develop an agent-based negotiation which can be seen as a decision-making process of resolving a conflict involving many parties over mutually goals.

In this example, we take contract suppliers, a logistic provider, and a retailer as our target members in the buyer-driven supply chain network of apparel industry (Figure 3.1). To demonstrate the proposed scheme, we used one apparel retailer as our sample case to entrust the third party logistic provider (*LP*) to fulfill the needs for the branded specialty retail. And the objective of *LP* is to find to several candidates which are contract suppliers with feasible alternatives through negotiation mechanism (In this study, the terms "buyer/seller" branded specialty retail/contract supplier and "retailer/supplier" are used interchangeably). After that, the *LP* and the retailer will use AHP to form the buyer-driven supply chain.

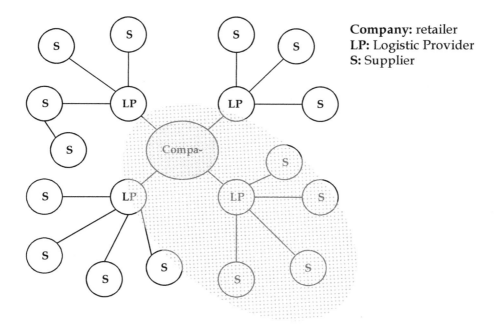

Company: retailer
LP: Logistic Provider
S: Supplier

Figure 3.1: The buyer-driven supply chain network.

In this lecture note, a novel approach is presented for the design of a buyer-driven supply chain. From the point of network design, for quick response of customer demands and maximum overall utility, the important issues are to find suitable and quality suppliers from multiple geographies, and to decide upon an appropriate production/distribution strategy. The proposed approach is based on the agent-based negotiation, and the analytical hierarchy process (AHP) to find the optimal combination and form the partnership in buyer-driven supply chain for the sake of gaining the most effective configuration. The proposed approach can provide the members selection and production/distribution planning for configuration design (Figure 3.2).

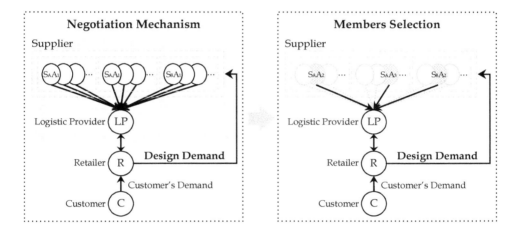

Figure 3.2: Production/distribution strategy for buyer-driven supply chain.

3.1.3   Research Contributions and Structure

Our main contribution of this lecture note is providing a platform which can negotiate not only quantitative attributes but also qualitative attributes employed fuzzy logic. And make this negotiation mechanism is more practical in a real world and worthy to implement. The rest of the lecture note is organized as follows. Section 3.2 briefly reviews some methodologies proposed of negotiation and AHP. And the details of the mechanism we proposed and the reasons that lie behind are given in section 3.3. The application is explained through apparel industry as our case study in section 3.4. Finally, the last section 3.5 contains some conclusions and perspectives.

3.2   Briefly Review of Methodologies

Buyer-driven supply network began in the late 1960s, direct foreign investment took a new tack; it supplemented its resource-seeking and market-seeking motives for globalization with a global search for cheap labor. This strategy by transnational firms coincided with the shift of developing countries from import-substituting industrialization (ISI) to export-oriented industrialization (EOI), which initially was facilitated by the growth of export-processing zones in many parts of the developing world (Grunwald & Flamm, 1985). In this study, we will use an example of apparel industry in Hong Kong to demonstrate buyer-driven supply chain.

In a buyer-driven supply chain, online trading becomes more common. A large number of digital marketplaces services are being developed, which offer more sophisticated trading environments. Software agent technologies are promising great advantages to the way we do in business (Jennings *et al.*, 2000), systems that use software agent technologies are proving to be effective in helping users make better decisions when buying or selling through the internet (Bailey & Bakos, 1997). Software agents can also play an important role in providing automation and support for the negotiation stage of online trading (Guttman, Moukas & Maes, 1997).

Negotiation is defined as a process by which a joint decision is made by two or more parties, the parties first verbalize contradictory demands and then move towards agreements (Pruitt, 1981; Sierra Faratin & Jennings, 2000). Most current digital marketplaces systems use predefined and non-adaptive negotiation strategies in the generation of offers and counter-offers during the course of negotiation (Wong, Zhang & Kara-Ali, 2000). For example, Kasbah is an electronic marketplace populated by selling and buying software agents who engage in a single issue negotiation (Maes, Guttman & Moukas, 1999). Experiments with Kasbah led to a design of Tête-à-Tête, a system capable of handling multi-issue negotiations (Maes *et al.*, 1999). Based on the users' issue weights, it constructs a rating function to evaluate offers made by other agents. Users may also specify bounds on the issue values which describe their reservation levels. So the first issue of our research is talking about that a successful negotiation which will occur when the two opposing offers meet, so the negotiation process consists of a number of decision-making process, each of which is characterized by evaluating an offer, determining strategies and generating a counter-offer (Bertsekas, 1995; Cyert & DeGroot, 1987; Zeng & Sycara, 1998).

Negotiation is a form of decision-making where two or more parties jointly explore possible solutions in order to reach a consensus (Rosenschein & Zlotkin, 1994). In common, negotiation can be classified according to the number of parities involved which can be one-to-one, one-to-many or many-to-many negotiation, and the number of attributes negotiated such as single-attribute or multiple-attributes (Rahwan, Kowalczyk & Pham, 2002). Our research supports one-to-many multi-attribute negotiation and its negotiation system architecture is shown in Figure 3.3 which illustrates two agents negotiate in the Internet through web server in digital market. And the detail of negotiation process will be described in the following section.

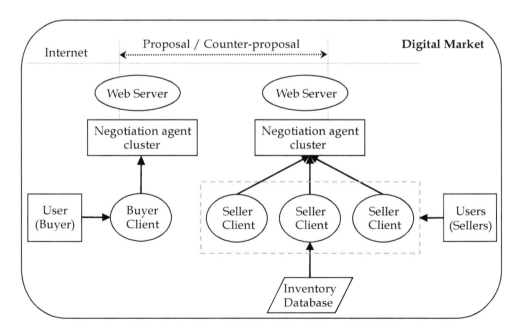

Figure 3.3: Negotiation system architecture.

Another issue is about supplier selection. In the literature, there are many studies about the supplier selection process. Traditional methodologies of the supplier selection process in research literature include the cost-ratio method, the categorical method, weighted-point evaluations, mathematical programming models and statistical or probabilistic approachs (Oliveria & Lourenço, 2002; Yan, Yu & Cheng, 2003). In this study, we implied analytic hierarchy process (AHP) to evaluate the alternatives obtained through negotiation mechanism, AHP is a powerful and flexible decision making process to help people set priorities and make the best decision when both qualitative and quantitative aspects of a decision need to be considered. By reducing complex decisions to a series of one-on-one comparisons, then synthesizing the results, AHP not only helps decision makers arrive at the best decision, but also provides a clear rationale that it is the best (Satty, 1977). AHP was also employed to arrive at the members selection of apparel industry for haute couture to find the partners to form a network integration.

3.3   Bilateral Negotiation and AHP (BiNA) Scheme

There are several basic members in apparel supply chain, from upstream to downstream, which are suppliers, logistic providers, and retailers, respectively. For our proposed Bilateral Negotiation and AHP (BiNA) scheme, we first take a logistic provider and suppliers through the negotiation mechanism to find out the alternatives which are determined by bilateral sides. After getting several alternatives, we use AHP to find the most optimal combination of members and form an integrated network.

As we know, our scheme mainly divided into two phases as shown in Figure 3.4, one is to execute how to proceed to one-to-many bilateral negotiation. In this part, we firstly do preliminary setting including negotiation parameters set and iso-curve computation which evaluate total scores of each alternative before starting negotiation. When entering negotiation, we proceed to select buyer's alternative based iso-curve from seller's proposal, consider seller's constraints to choose buyer's alternative. Consequently, using attributes trade-off to get several potential alternatives which are negotiated by buyer agent and seller agent. The second phase is using AHP to select the best association of members which can bring the great performance and effectiveness in buyer-driven supply chain.

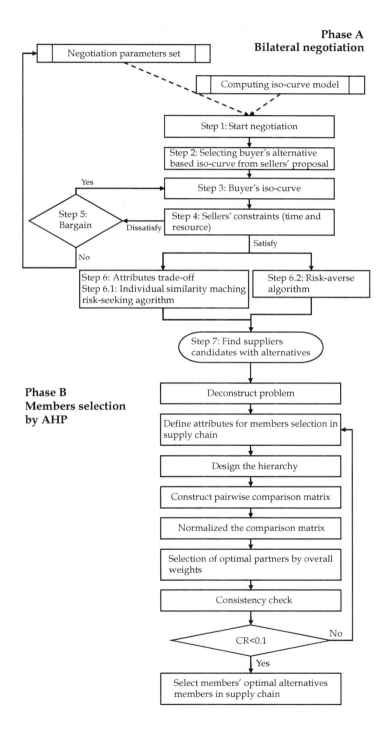

Figure 3.4: BiNA scheme.

In this section, we first introduce some definitions which are needed in our BiNA scheme, then present the process of negotiation and AHP step by step. And some definitions are shown as following subsections:

3.3.1   Negotiation Parameters Set

There are i sellers will be chosen from buyer for the key component. We discuss there are n attributes (a_j) discussed about this key component.

Definition 1 Buyer generates several feasible alternatives $(a_{a_j}^B)$ by its own set of attributes $([a_{a_1}^B, a_{a_2}^B, ..., a_{a_n}^B])$, which include quantitative and qualitative attributes, at the same iso-curve value which is shown in Definition 5. And buyer's range of attribute $(a_{a_1}^B\_lower, a_{a_1}^B\_upper)$, seller's range of attribute $(a_{a_1}^{S_i}\_lower, a_{a_1}^{S_i}\_upper)$, and the negotiation times are all determined by themselves.

$$a_{a_j}^B = \left[a_{a_1}^B, a_{a_2}^B, ..., a_{a_n}^B \right].$$

At first, each seller (S_i) also will offer their own set of attributes $(a_{a_j}^{S_i})$ to buyer.

$$a_{a_j}^{S_i} = \left[a_{a_1}^{S_i}, a_{a_2}^{S_i}, ..., a_{a_n}^{S_i} \right].$$

Definition 2 The weights determined by buyer $(W_{a_j}^B)$ and sellers $(W_{a_j}^{S_i})$ for n attributes (a_j); weights are from 0 to 1:

$$W_{a_j}^B : [W_{a_1}^B, W_{a_2}^B, ..., W_{a_n}^B]$$

$$W_{a_j}^{S_i} : [W_{a_1}^{S_i}, W_{a_2}^{S_i}, ..., W_{a_n}^{S_i}]$$

$$\sum_{j=1}^{n} W_{a_j}^B = 1, \quad \sum_{j=1}^{n} W_{a_j}^{S_i} = 1$$

Evaluating Attributes in negotiation is a key role when solving process. However, in evaluating process, each attribute has its different scale to describe and divides into quantitative and qualitative attributes. To solve this problem, we applied membership functions in fuzzy logic which are determined by buyer and sellers, and using fuzzy value to normalize different scales between all attributes and make them have the same scale.

Definition 3 Fuzzy value can be perceived as the mean to measure the degree of compatibility of a quantitative attribute value to a fuzzy set. A triangular number (a, b, c) is a fuzzy set that has a membership function of the following form:

$$\mu(x) = \begin{cases} \dfrac{x-a}{b-a} &, \quad \text{if } x < a \\ \dfrac{c-x}{c-b} &, \quad \text{if } a \le x < b \\ 1 &, \quad \text{if } x \ge b \end{cases} \tag{10}$$

In addition, triangular numbers also provide qualitative attributives that may be given by means of the fuzzy singleton (Castro-Schez1, Jennings, Luo & Shadbolt, 2004) shown in Figure 3.5(a) to (c). For instance, whether the outsourced item is with service or not is Boolean type attribute, and specification of the item can be ranked by buyer/seller preference which is ranking with order type attribute. Each value is expressed by the fuzzy singleton that is determined from formula (11).

In order to better facilitate interaction between the user and software agent from a practical viewpoint, we then employed triangular membership function to determine the user linguistic value of each quantitative/qualitative attribute. When the fuzzy membership function of each attribute is decided, we can then convert these human linguistic values of attributes into fuzzy value $(FV_{a_1}^B(FV_{a_1}^{S_i}))$. And Table 3.1 shows the notations of fuzzy value of buyer (seller) through fuzzy membership function.

3.3.2 Computing Iso-curve Model

In negotiation, buyer agent and seller agent can send not only reject or accept message of proposal (alternative), but also evaluation of their alternatives $(a_{a_j}^B(a_{a_j}^{S_i}))$. In this subsection, we use iso-curve model to evaluate total scores of each alternative which is formed by a set of attributes.

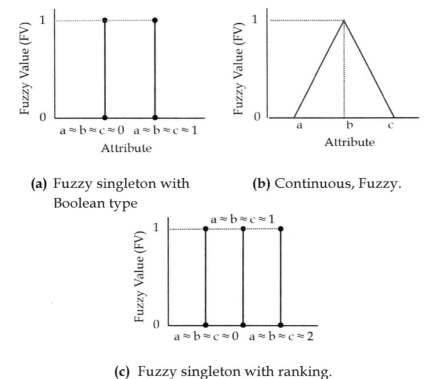

(a) Fuzzy singleton with Boolean type

(b) Continuous, Fuzzy.

(c) Fuzzy singleton with ranking.

Figure 3.5: Various continuous/discrete attribute types that triangular membership numbers can represent.

Attribute	Attribute value of Buyer (Seller)	Fuzzy value of Buyer (Seller)
a_j	$a_{a_j}^B$ $(a_{a_j}^{S_i})$	$FV_{a_1}^B$ $(FV_{a_1}^{S_i})$

Table 3.1: Fuzzy value for different scale of each attribute.

Definition 4 Total scores (TS_{a_j}) of an alternative which is made up by weights W_{a_j} $(W^B_{a_1}(W^{S_i}_{a_1}))$ and fuzzy value FV_{a_j} $(FV^B_{a_1}(FV^{S_i}_{a_1}))$ for attribute a_j is formulated as:

$$TS = \left(\sum_{j=1}^{n} W_{a_j} \times (FV_{a_j}) \right)^{\frac{1}{r}} \tag{12}$$

where r represents the value from $-\infty$ to ∞, a spectrum total score models such as *Minimum, Weighted arithmetic mean,* and *Maximum etc.* (Dujmovic, 1975; Su *et al.*, 2001). Some commonly used functions are given in Table 3.2. The total score models can be selected by a user to suit different decision situations and for the selection of different attributes.

Total Score Models	Function	r value
Minimum model	$TS = \min(FV_{a_1}, FV_{a_2}, \cdots, FV_{a_n})$	$r = -\infty$
Harmonic mean model	$TS = 1 / \sum_{j=1}^{n} (W_{a_j} / FV_{a_j})$	$r = -1$
Geometric mean model	$TS = (FV_{a_1})^{W_{a_1}} \cdot (FV_{a_2})^{W_{a_2}} \cdots (FV_{a_n})^{W_{a_n}}$	$r = 0$
Weighted arithmetic mean model	$TS = \sum_{j=1}^{n} W_{a_j} \times FV_{a_j}$	$r = 1$
Square mean model	$TS = \sqrt{\sum_{j=1}^{n} W_{a_j} \times (FV_{a_j})^2}$	$r = 2$
Maximum model	$TS = \max(FV_{a_1}, FV_{a_2}, \cdots, FV_{a_n})$	$r = \infty$

Table 3.2: Total score model types.

Here using different total score *models will lead to different results*, so it depends on users' decision toward which attribute prefers more. During the negotiation process, buyer agent will generate some potential alternatives that is the same total score value as the previous one offered, but expecting to be more acceptable the other alternatives with different attributes combination for its seller agents The generating method is initiated by first generating new alternatives that lie on what is called the *iso-value curve* which derived from the next definition (Raiffa, 1982). In this study, we use iso-curve in the bargain step. When the alternative firstly proposed which lies on some iso-curve don't fit in with the range set up by sellers, the buyer will lower iso-curve value to the next level.

Definition 5 An iso-curve is defined as the curve formed by all the proposals with the same total score values for buyer agent. Given a score d, the iso-curve set at degree d_k (in the k level) for buyer's alternative $a_{a_j}^B$ is defined as:

$$iso(d_k) = \{a_{a_j}^B \mid TS_{a_j}^B = d_k\} \tag{13}$$

3.4   Similarity Matching

In our study, we use similarity matching to support sellers easily find more suitable alternative of buyer because of different cognitions for attributes between both sides. There are two kinds of similarity evaluation, which are *united similarity* for each alternative and *individual similarity* for each attribute respectively.

United similarity matching is used when buyer agent receives seller's proposals first, it will use *united similarity* to match its own and sellers' alternatives to find out one set of attributes which has the largest similarity with each seller.

Definition 6 *United similarity* between buyer and sellers for alternative ($a_{a_j}^B$ ($a_{a_j}^{S_i}$)) is defined as:

$$Sim_{a_j}^{B,S_i} = \frac{\sum W_{a_j}^{B,S_i} \times S_{a_j}^{B,S_i}}{\sum W_{a_j}^{B,S_i}}, \tag{14}$$

where

$$W_{a_j}^{B,S_i} = \sqrt{W_{a_j}^B \times W_{a_j}^{S_i}}$$

represents joint weights of buyer and sellers for attribute a_j and $a_{a_j}^{B,S_i}$ represents the similarity degree of buyer and sellers for attribute a_j which can be divided into computing quantified attributes:

$$S_{a_j}^{B,S_i} = 1 - \frac{\left| a_{a_j}^{B} - a_{a_j}^{S_i} \right|}{\max\{a_{a_j}^{B}, a_{a_j}^{S_i}\}}$$

and qualified attributes:

$$S_{a_j}^{B,S_i} = \begin{cases} 1, & \text{if } u_{a_j}^{S_i}(a_{a_j}^{S_i}) \leq u_{a_j}^{S_i}(a_{a_j}^{B}) \\ 1 - [u_{a_j}^{S_i}(a_{a_j}^{S_i}) - u_{a_j}^{S_i}(a_{a_j}^{B})], & \text{otherwise} \end{cases} \text{, where } 0 \leq u \leq 1$$

Buyer will offer a counter-proposal to each seller, at this time, each seller will check and match each attribute in buyer's alternative offered. And they will use *individual similarity* to do matching.

Definition 7 *Individual similarity* between each attribute a_j of buyer and sellers' alternatives is defined as:

$$Sim_{a_j}^{B,S_i} = \frac{W_{a_j}^{B,S_i} \times S_{a_j}^{B,S_i}}{W_{a_j}^{B,S_i}} \tag{15}$$

3.5   BiNA Procedure in Buyer-driven Supply Chain

After knowing the definitions of negotiation, in this subsection, we start to propose our research through two phases of the scheme. The first phase will be described by the following negotiation steps to evaluate the alternatives among involvers within supply chain. We present how to execute our negotiation mechanism which mainly classified five parts as shown in Figure 3.6. We firstly defined negotiation parameters set and iso-curve computation in *Preliminary setting*. Secondly, *Negotiation alternative processing service* will be proposed to select buyer's alternative based on iso-curve. After selecting negotiation alternative, buyer agent will send its alternative (counter-proposal) to seller agents to determine if it satisfies seller's constraints or not then decide *iso-curve relaxation*. Consequently, we use *Trade-off* strategies to find some potential alternatives for the offers of outsourcing partners. At the second phase which is selecting members' alternatives in the buyer-driven supply network using AHP. Here we will also introduce AHP procedures to evaluate partners to form supply chain for the LP offers of configuring partners.

3.5.1   Phase A (Bilateral negotiation): Find Out Appropriate Alternatives between Sellers and Buyer through Negotiation

Step A1. Start negotiation

Each seller agent proposes an alternative ($a_{a_j}^{S_i}$) to buyer agent.

Step A2. Selecting buyer's alternative based iso-curve from sellers' proposal

When receiving each seller agent's alternative, buyer agent starts to proceed to united similarity matching using formula (14). Find an alternative of buyer agent ($a_{a_j}^B$) which has the largest similarity with all seller agents.

Step A3. Buyer's iso-curve values

In this step, buyer agent sends a counter-proposal (alternative $a_{a_j}^B$ from *Step2*) using iso-curve back to each seller agent.

Step A4. Sellers' constraints (time and resource)

When each seller agent receives the counter-proposal (alternative $a_{a_j}^B$) from buyer agent, it uses mathematical constraints to decide if the alternative $a_{a_j}^B$ satisfies seller's own limitation of time and resource or not. About time limitation, if negotiation times between buyer and seller agents exceed default negotiation times, and then this negotiation fails.

Moreover, about resource limitation, if the attributes in buyer agent's alternative satisfies seller's constraints, and then goes to *Step5*; if dissatisfies, and then goes to *Step6*.

Please refer to Algorithm 1 for detail.

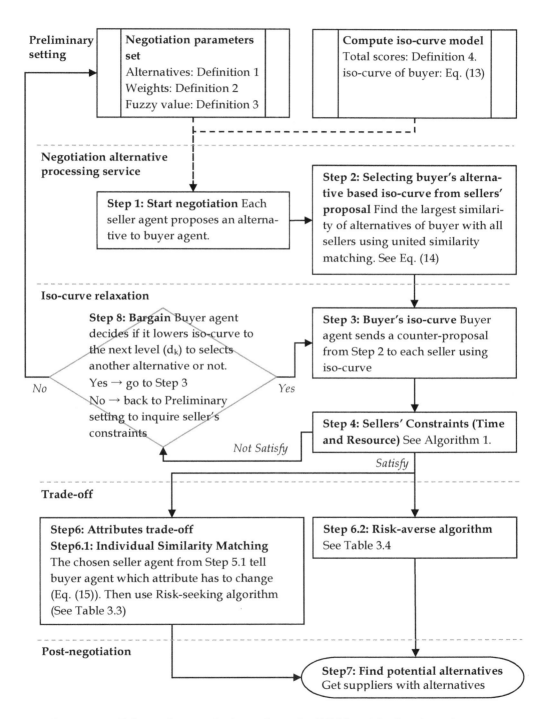

Figure 3.6: Bilateral negotiation phase in BiNA – Mechanism for negotiation procedure.

> *If nego_time ≤ default nego_time*
> > *If count_proposal ∈ a_j's range of sellers (∀a_j)*
> > > *Then satisfy and go to Step5*
> > *Else*
> > > *dissatisfy and go to Step6*
> > *End if*
> *Else*
> > *negotiation fails*
> *End if*

Algorithm 1: Sellers' constraints (time and resource) for Step A4.

Step A5. Bargain

When buyer agent receives dissatisfy message from *Step4*, it will decide to whether alternative relax iso-curve or not. If yes, then go to *Step3* to lower iso-value to the next level (d_k) and select another alternative as the following fuzzy rules. We takes the attributes discussed as our inputs which are modeled by fuzzy sets with *j* items, and one output, iso-curve Lowering Degree (LD), which is modeled by iso-curve value according to concession degree. Due to fuzzy rules decided by buyer, if buyer does not lower its iso-curve, then go back to *Preliminary setting* (Figure 3.6) to inquire seller's constraints then proceed with the following steps. And the fuzzy rule is shown as follows:

$$\text{If } a_j \text{ is } T_j, \text{ then LD is } d_k,$$

where a_j (*j* = 1, 2, …) means attribute and T_j (*j* = 1, 2, …) is the item which is described buyer's linguistic values for the attributes. And d_k ($k = 0,1,2,...$) stands for iso-curve value in *k* level of buyer's concession degree.

Step A6. Attributes trade-off

The trade-off rules are according to two kinds of strategies toward risk (risk-seeking, and risk-averse), which are determined by buyer's attitude toward risk. And each strategy is also subdivided into *Cost-oriented* and

Benefit-oriented respectively. For instance, the attribute *Price* for buyer agent is the lower the better, so it is classified as *Cost-oriented*. However, for attribute *Quantity* which is the more the better for buyer agent, so it is sorted as *Benefit-oriented*

Step A6.1. Risk-seeking strategy

In this step, each seller agent first uses individual similarity matching which can let buyer agent know which attribute have to change. After individual similarity matching, we use risk-seeking strategy (shown in Table 3.3) to cope with attributes trade-off corresponding to the largest unsimilarity between buyer agent and seller agent.

Cost-oriented for buyer	**Benefit-oriented for buyer**
When $a_{a_1}^{S_i}\_upper \geq a_{a_1}^{B}\_lower$ If $a_{a_1}^{S_i}\_lower \leq a_{a_j}^{B'} \leq a_{a_1}^{B}\_upper$ then accept $a_{a_j}^{B'}$ else deal $\leftarrow a_{a_1}^{S_i}\_lower$ end if	When $a_{a_1}^{B}\_lower \geq a_{a_1}^{S_i}\_upper$ If $a_{a_1}^{B}\_lower \leq a_{a_j}^{B'} \leq a_{a_1}^{S_i}\_upper$ then accept $a_{a_j}^{B'}$ else deal $\leftarrow a_{a_1}^{S_i}\_upper$ end if

Table 3.3: Risk-seeking strategy in attributes trade-off.

For Cost-oriented:
(Buyer agent and seller agents all have their own ranges for attribute a_j). If one of the attributes in buyer's alternative ($a_{a_j}^{B'}$) is within the range between seller's lower bound ($a_{a_1}^{B'}\_lower$) and buyer's upper bound ($a_{a_1}^{B}\_upper$) for attribute a_j, and then accept this value ($a_{a_j}^{B'}$). Else, seller's lower bound is a deal.

For Benefit-oriented:
If one of the attributes in buyer's alternative ($a_{a_j}^{B'}$) is within the range between buyer's lower bound and seller's upper bound ($a_{a_1}^{S_j}\_upper$) for attribute a_j, and then accept this value ($a_{a_j}^{B'}$). Else, seller's upper bound is a deal.

Step A6.2. Risk-averse strategy

We already know the alternative of the chosen seller, and then we use risk-averse strategy to proceed with attributes trade-off. The trade-off strategies are determined by buyer as shown in Figure 3.7. And buyer's attitudes to trade-off can be classified to "anxious", "cool-head", and "frugal" (Maes *et al.*, 1999).

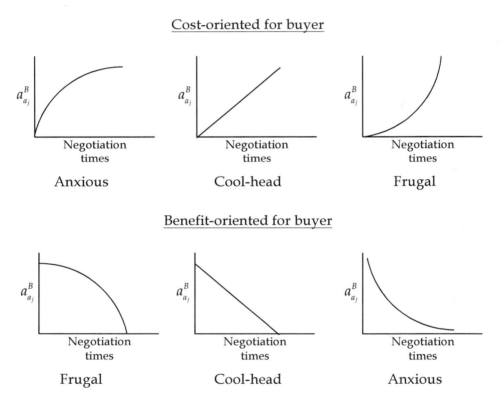

Figure 3.7: Trade-off strategies.

Because buyer agent wants to keep the same level d_k of iso-curve ($iso(d_k)$), we next used mathematical programming to calculate buyer's new alternative based on buyer and seller's initial requirements. Table 3.4 shows risk-averse strategy in attributes trade-off.

Cost-oriented for buyer	Benefit-oriented for buyer
Objective: $iso(d_k)$ keeps the same	Objective: $iso(d_k)$ keeps the same
Constraint: $a_{a_j}^{S_i} \le a_{a_j}^{B'} \le a_{a_j}^{B}$	Constraint: $a_{a_j}^{S_i} \le a_{a_j}^{B'} \le a_{a_j}^{B}$

Table 3.4 Risk-averse strategy in trade-off.

Step A7. Find the potential alternatives determined by buyer and seller

After above steps, this step can get some alternatives with buyer and sellers' consensus. So these alternatives will be used to choose when entering into next phase.

3.5.2   Phase B (Members selection by AHP): Partners with Alternatives in Supply Chain Selection using AHP

From the aforementioned negotiation procedures, there are several alternatives between members in buyer-driven supply chain. Here, we use AHP in multi-criteria decision-making (MDCM) approach to decide the optimal combination and form the partnership in supply chain for the sake of gaining the most effective configuration (Figure 3.8).

The process of AHP is firstly deconstructing problem then defining attributes for members with alternatives selection and proceed with designing the hierarchy of those attributes (see formula (1)~(7)). After the former steps in determining some parameters, we enter the evaluating steps which are constructing and normalizing pair-wise comparison matrix. Consequently, there will be some partners with alternatives which are negotiated in advance chosen and compose an integrated supply chain.

3.6   Example Demonstration

In this example, we take contract suppliers, a logistic provider, and a retailer as our target members in buyer-driven supply network of apparel industry (Figure 3.9). To demonstrate the proposed BiNA scheme, we used one apparel retailer (*PH corp.*) as our sample case. It sells *haute couture* for certain designer brand in Hong Kong. And *PH corp.* entrust the third party logistic provider (*LP*) to fulfill the needs for the whole process of clothing

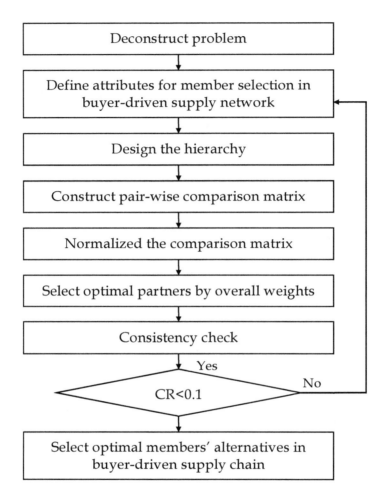

Figure 3.8 Members selection phase in BiNA – AHP procedure.

which are spinning, weaving, dyeing, cutting, and sewing. And the objective of *LP* is to find to several candidates for the clothing processes which are suppliers with feasible alternatives through negotiation mechanism. After that, the third party logistic provider (*LP*) and the apparel retailer (*PH corp.*) will use AHP to choose the network formed by triple sides of the suppliers, *PH corp.*, and *LP*.

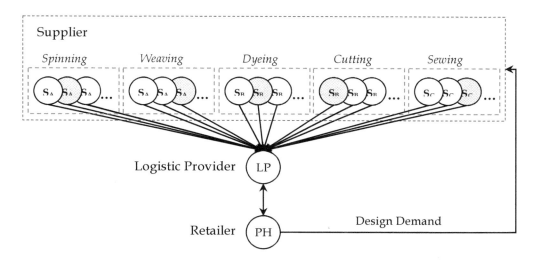

Figure 3.9 The buyer-driven supply chain in apparel industry.

For the first phase of negotiation mechanism, we take two cutting suppliers and the logistic provider as our object to proceed to bilateral negotiation, and also known as the other suppliers of clothing process, to use the same mechanism with the logistic provider. In this study, these two cutting suppliers will be evaluated and named as Supplier A (from China) and Supplier B (from Malaysia). With this basic background about the suppliers, we start our negotiation mechanism processes step by step.

Table 3.5 shows the set of attributes involved in negotiation for the logistic provider (*LP*), Cutting Supplier A, and Cutting Supplier B respectively. It details the ranges of acceptable values, fuzzy value and the weights used to signify the level of importance for attributes, which are *Style*, *Delivery Time*, and *Price*. The attribute *Style* is qualitatively subdivided into three standards which are *High fashion*, *Classical*, and *Comfortable*. Consumers who have different preferences about cutting professional skills will lead to distinct purchasing behaviors. So the specialty skills' experience of these three styles was evaluated in cutting supplier members. Moreover, we consider other two quantitative attributes, *Delivery Time* and *Price*, which are also concerned the most by buyers.

After we know the basic information, the logistic provider (*LP*) agent and the supplier agents start to negotiate with each other.

	Buyer: Logistic Provider (LP)			Cutting Supplier A			Cutting Supplier B		
	Range	Fuzzy Value	Weights	Range	Fuzzy Value	Weights	Range	Fuzzy Value	Weights
Style	High fashion	0	0.35	High fashion	0	0.3	High fashion	0	0.3
	Classic	1		Classic	2		Classic	1	
	Comfortable	2		Comfortable	1		Comfortable	2	
Delivery Time (Weeks)	[1, 6]	[0.9, 0.4]	0.2	[2,6]	[0.5, 0.7]	0.5	[4,8]	[0.6, 0.8]	0.3
Price ($/batch)	[3000, 5000]	[0.8, 0.4]	0.45	[4000,5750]	[0.45, 0.8]	0.2	[3000,3750]	[0.25, 0.5]	0.4

Table 3.5 LP/Suppliers' weights and their fuzzy value for all attributes.

First of all, each supplier agent sends to *LP* agent an alternative; Supplier A offers a cutting with comfortable style and delivering by 4 weeks for a price $5500 per batch, [Comfortable, 4, 5500] which is named as *Proposal_A_1*. And Supplier B offers *Proposal_B_1* [Classical, 5, 3750] to *LP* agent. And the total scores of the two alternatives for agents of Supplier A and Supplier B, which chooses weighted arithmetic mean model from Table 3.2, are 0.56 and 0.415 respectively.

Then, *LP* agent generates a set of iso-curve alternatives and find out *Counter-Proposal_1* [Comfortable, 6, 2000] which has the most united similarity with two supplier agents using formula (14). So *LP* agent sends this alternative back (also named counter-proposal) to each supplier agent.

Because *LP's Price* ($2000) falls neither Supplier A nor Supplier B's range for the attribute *Price*, *LP* agent must lower the iso-curve value to the next level and determine another alternative until satisfying suppliers' constraints. So we need to use fuzzy inference rules as our bargain strategy. We takes the attributes as our inputs which are modeled by fuzzy sets with three items, and one output which is modeled by iso-curve value according to concession degree.

The fuzzy inference method is used as follows:

- *Input 1:* Style (S) = {important (I), neutral (N), unimportant (UI)}

- *Input 2:* Delivery Time (DT) = {important (I), neutral (N), unimportant (UI)}

- *Input 3:* Price (P) = {important (I), neutral (N), unimportant (UI)

- *Output:* iso-curve Lowering Degree (LD) = {same level (d_0), lower 1 level (d_1), lower 2 levels (d_2)}

The corresponding membership function is shown in Figure 3.10. In this step, we use fuzzy inference rules to describe buyer's concession degree for the attributes as Table 3.6.

Consequently, *LP* agent offers each supplier agent *Counter-Proposal_2* [Comfortable, 5, 3300] according to the above fuzzy rules. In the next step, each supplier agent uses individual similarity matching to let *LP* agent know the attribute *Price* has to change. And *LP* agent first uses risk-seeking as its changing strategy. Because *Price* is the lower the better for *LP*, it chooses cost-oriented as its attributes trade-off strategy. In the end, a final agreement [Comfortable, 5, 3300] achieves through trade-off between *LP* and each supplier for cutting.

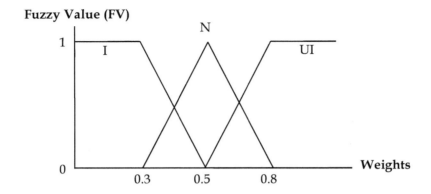

Figure 3.10: Membership function for the attributes.

Rules	If S	and DT	and P	Then LD	Rules	If S	and DT	and P	Then LD
1	I	I	I	d_0	15	N	N	UI	d_1
2	I	I	N	d_0	16	N	UI	I	d_1
3	I	I	UI	d_1	17	N	UI	N	d_1
4	I	N	I	d_0	18	N	UI	UI	d_2
5	I	N	N	d_0	19	UI	I	I	d_1
6	I	N	UI	d_1	20	UI	I	N	d_1
7	I	UI	I	d_1	21	UI	I	UI	d_2
8	I	UI	N	d_1	22	UI	N	I	d_1
9	I	UI	UI	d_1	23	UI	N	N	d_1
10	N	I	I	d_0	24	UI	N	UI	d_2
11	N	I	N	d_0	25	UI	UI	I	d_1
12	N	I	UI	d_1	26	UI	UI	N	d_2
13	N	N	I	d_0	27	UI	UI	UI	d_2
14	N	N	N	d_1					

Table 3.6: Fuzzy rules of buyer's concession degree for the attributes.

Then, *LP* agent uses risk-averse strategy with cool-head attitude as its trade-off strategy. In the end, a final agreement of Supplier A and B are [Classical, 3, 4750] and [Comfortable, 4, 3000] respectively through trade-off between the logistic provider (*LP*) and Supplier B for cutting. The negotiation mechanism of agents for the logistic provider and Supplier A, B can also be illustrated as Figure 3.11.

After proceeding with forementioned steps, we will get four negotiation processes of each quantitative attribute using different trade-off strategies between *LP* and Supplier A and B in Table 3.7. Then we compare each alternative's performance for *LP* using AHP to give the retailer's manager advice to manage.

From Table 3.7, we could conclude that when adopting the risk-seeking strategy given both sellers, the negotiation would end in one time for each attribute. Because when company wants to use risk-seeking strategy, and that means this company likes to risk on trade-off. This manner will cause two extreme results, either beneficial or losing. Strategies choosing depends on managers attitudes toward trade-off in the market. And the above negotiation process can form four sets of attributes which are style, delivery time, and price (Table 3.8). These four alternatives are potential combinations negotiated by *LP* and two suppliers based on two different strategies.

After knowing the alternatives combined with *LP* and Supplier A and B, we proceed to the second phase which is AHP for *members with the alternatives selection*. Then, four alternatives will be evaluated subsequently. These four alternatives are composed by negotiating between *LP* and two Supplier A and B and which are used two different trade-off strategies, risk-seeking and risk-averse. With this basic background about the alternatives, we started our members selection mechanism process step by step.

The objective of members selection is to choose the optimal one for cutting providers and develop it to gain the most benefits for the retailer. So when we start to select, we firstly decide which attributes are needed to evaluate alternatives. These attributes have equitable and objective factors to choose the optimal combination of the retailer and certain cutting supplier. And Figure 3.12 shows the hierarchy of selecting these four alternatives.

To begin this phase, we met with the retailer and the logistic provider to jointly determine which attribute was the most important to them in

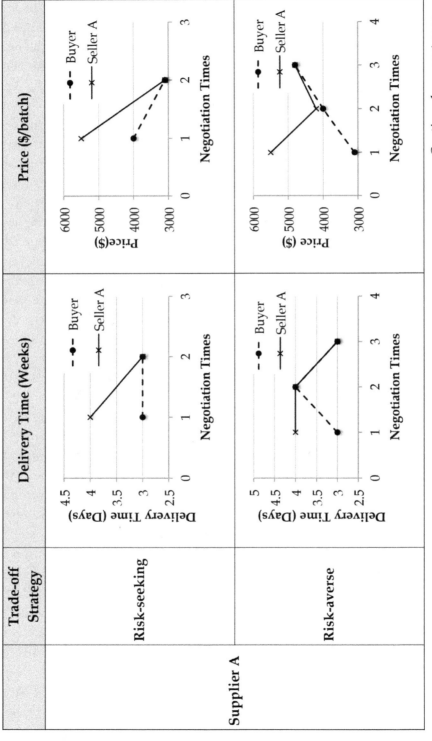

Continued on next page...

... Continued from previous page

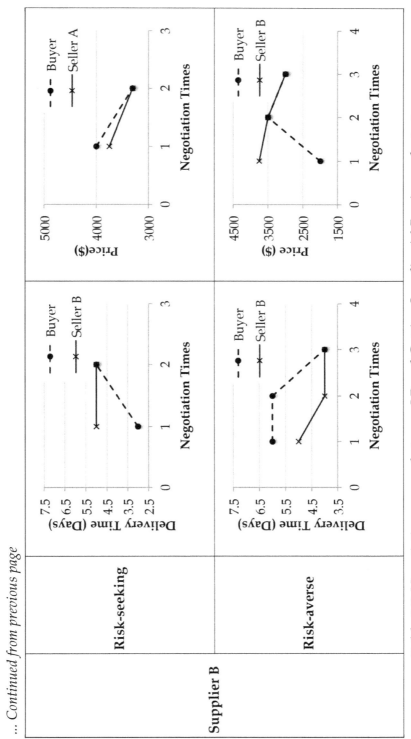

Table 3.7: Negotiation process between LP and Cutting Supplier A&B using each strategy.

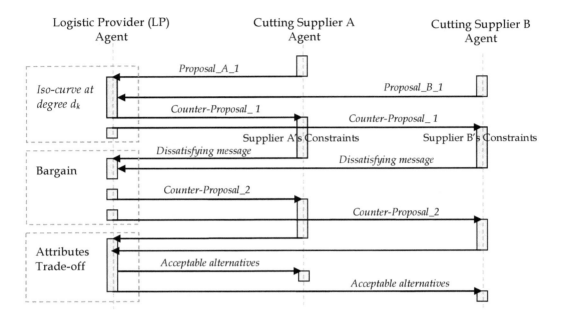

Figure 3.11 Negotiation mechanism of agents for *LP* and Supplier A and B.

Alternatives attributes	Supplier A Alternative 1 (S_AA_1)	Supplier A Alternative 2 (S_AA_2)	Supplier B Alternative 1 (S_BA_1)	Supplier B Alternative 2 (S_BA_2)
Different Strategies of Suppliers	Supplier A (risk-seeking)	Supplier A (risk-averse)	Supplier B (risk-seeking)	Supplier B (risk-averse)
Style	Comfortable	Classical	Classical	Comfortable
Delivery Time (Weeks)	3	3	5	4
Price ($/batch)	3100	4750	3300	3000

Table 3.8: The initial offers of each attribute between two suppliers for cutting.

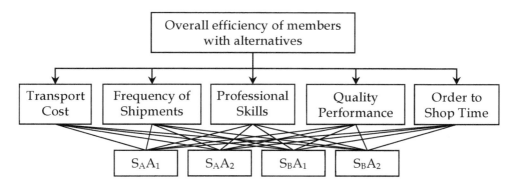

Figure 3.12 The hierarchy of members with alternatives selection.

choosing members with alternatives. We arrived at five quantitative and qualitative attributes which were Transport Cost, Frequency of Shipments, Replenishment Policy, IT Communication, and Order to Shop Time. In this sample case, there were two suppliers with two alternatives to choose from which are S_AA_1, S_AA_2, S_BA_1, S_BA_2, and we used five attributes to analyze the performance of each alternative. In Table 3.8, the alternatives' information in relation to these attributes negotiated is listed for the cutting part.

At this point in this phase, the retailer and the logistic provider's managers were asked to prioritize the five attributes in view of the alternatives' performances to generate the accompanies matrix. This is done by using pair-wise comparison with Saaty's 1–9 scales (Figure 2.2). To compute each alternative's weights, one need is to calculate the overall priority. Overall priority is calculated by multiplying the respective terms in priority of *attributes* by *the priority of decision alternatives*. And Table 3.9~3.12 shows the process of constructing the pair-wise comparison matrices and their normalized process with the attributes "Transport Cost" as an example, and the same steps used to compute the other attributes. To facilitate AHP calculation, Matlab® programming utilities were used.

After repeating this calculation for each of the five attributes, the last step in the selection process is to calculate the final rank of potential alternatives for the outsourced component. The members with alternatives selection results are shown in Table 3.13.

$$O_s =$$

	Transport Cost	Frequency of Shipments	Professional Skills	Quality Performance	Order to Shop Time
Transport Cost	1	5	5	7	3
Frequency of Shipments	1/5	1	3	1/3	1/5
Professional Skills	1/5	1/3	1	3	1/5
Quality Performance	1/7	3	1/3	1	1/7
Order to Shop Time	1/3	5	5	7	1

Table 3.9: Initial comparison matrix of attributes among the suppliers.

$$O_A =$$

	S_AA_1	S_AA_2	S_BA_1	S_BA_2
S_AA_1	1	5	5	1/3
S_AA_2	1/5	1	1/3	1/5
S_BA_1	1/5	3	1	1/5
S_BA_2	3	5	5	1

Table 3.10: Initial comparison matrix of attributes "Transport Cost".

	Transport Cost	Frequency of Shipments	Professional Skills	Quality Performance	Order to Shop Time
Transport Cost	1	5	5	7	3
Frequency of Shipments	1/5	1	3	1/3	1/5
Professional Skills	1/5	1/3	1	3	1/5
Quality Performance	1/7	3	1/3	1	1/7
Order to Shop Time	1/3	5	5	7	1

$O_s =$ (left of the first table)

↓ Normalized

	Transport Cost	Frequency of Shipments	Professional Skills	Quality Performance	Order to Shop Time
Transport Cost	0.5330	0.3488	0.3488	0.3818	0.6604
Frequency of Shipments	0.1066	0.0698	0.2093	0.0182	0.0440
Replenishment Policy	0.1066	0.0233	0.0698	0.1636	0.0440
IT Communication	0.0761	0.2093	0.0233	0.0545	0.0314
Order to Shop Time	0.1777	0.3488	0.3488	0.3818	0.2201

$O_s =$ (left of the second table)

Table 3.11: Normalized comparison matrix of each attribute among the alternatives.

$$O_A =$$

	S_AA_1	S_AA_2	S_BA_1	S_BA_2
S_AA_1	1	2	5	3
S_AA_2	1/2	1	5	3
S_BA_1	1/5	1/5	1	1/3
S_BA_2	1/3	1/3	3	1

↓ Normalized

$$O_A =$$

	S_AA_1	S_AA_2	S_BA_1	S_BA_2
S_AA_1	0.2273	0.3571	0.4412	0.1923
S_AA_2	0.0455	0.0714	0.0294	0.1154
S_BA_1	0.0455	0.2143	0.0882	0.1154
S_BA_2	0.6818	0.3571	0.4412	0.5769

Table 3.12: Normalized initial comparison matrix of attributes "Transport Cost".

Suppliers with alternatives	Weights
Supplier A with alternative 1 (S_AA_1)	0.3045
Supplier A with alternative 2 (S_AA_2)	0.0654
Supplier B with alternative 1 (S_BA_1)	0.1158
Supplier B with alternative 2 (S_BA_2)	**0.5143**

Table 3.13: Members selection results.

Based on the results for overall weights in Phase B, we recommended Supplier B as the most favorable cutting supplier for the retailer. And its alternative is with Comfortable style and delivery for 4 days for the price $3000 per batch. And we can adopt exact the same process on the other suppliers of clothing processes as we mentioned above, which are selected by the retailer and the logistic provider jointly. So the whole clothing providers' overall rank is shown in Table 3.14 and 3.15.

Spinning Suppliers	Weights (W_S)	Weaving Suppliers	Weights (W_S)	Dyeing Suppliers	Weights (W_S)
Supplier A with alt. 1	0.1368	Supplier A with alt. 1	0.3002	Supplier A with alt. 1	0.2685
Supplier A with alt. 2	0.2410	Supplier A with alt. 2	0.1543	Supplier A with alt. 2	0.0142
Supplier B with alt. 1	0.4211	Supplier B with alt. 1	0.0245	Supplier B with alt. 1	0.1375
Supplier B with alt. 2	0.2011	Supplier B with alt. 2	0.0097	Supplier B with alt. 2	0.1102
		Supplier C with alt. 1	0.2474	Supplier C with alt. 1	0.2753
		Supplier C with alt. 2	0.2639	Supplier C with alt. 2	0.1943

Table 3.14: Weights for all members in supply chain for apparel industry.

Supplier A with alt. 1	0.3045	Supplier A with alt. 1	0.1849
Supplier A with alt. 2	0.0654	Supplier A with alt. 2	0.3555
Supplier B with alt. 1	0.1158	Supplier B with alt. 1	0.2035
Supplier B with alt. 2	0.5143	Supplier B with alt. 2	0.2561

Table 3.15: Weights for all members in supply chain for apparel industry (continue).

After obtaining weights of each member from the processing of raw materials to the production of the finished goods in apparel industry, we can form a network among the suppliers, the retailer and the logistic provider (Figure 3.13).

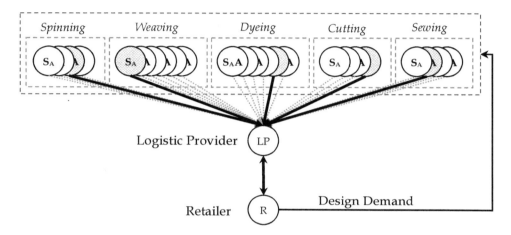

Figure 3.13 The network among the suppliers, the retailer and the logistic provider.

Through the whole process above, we acquire a network of members which form an integral supply chain and collaborated suppliers which have the best preferences evaluated by the retailer and the logistic provider.

Because we already gain several alternatives along with certain suppliers in Phase A, we can get not only the members form the whole supply chain, but also can get their alternatives in Phase B. In the first phase, the retailer gives design demands for the clothing and entrust the logistic provider to find the suppliers for those demands. After having some candidates for the suppliers, then the retailer can use AHP to find which have the good achievements based consumers' requirements in the second phase. Therefore, the retailer can get the suppliers from the processing of raw materials to the production of the finished goods through the third party logistic provider and compose the integrated supply chain in apparel industry.

3.7   Brief Summary

Negotiation recently was developing dramatically and very important to the success for every industry. This is because the cost and quality of goods and services are usually concerned by buyers and need to negotiate. Therefore, we propose a mechanism of one-to-many bilateral negotiation in this research. Sellers and buyers in agent-based supply chain through negotiations have significant impact on supplier selection and partners' profit. Using the fuzzy value in fuzzy logic transfers linguistic value into the same scale in order to evaluate sequent process. Then through the communications between buyer's and sellers' agents to let both sides know opponents' behavior and decide which trade-off strategy can be implied. Among the negotiation, similarity matching applied in two parts; one is to find the most similar alternative as the counter-proposal of buyer, the other is for buyer to choose a business partner and know which attributes has to change and make a consensus with seller. This negotiation contributed more practical approach; because it included fuzzy logic to represent the attributes and jointed buyer's behavior within negotiation, therefore, this research makes close to negotiate in a real world.

And we also use Analytic Hierarchy Process (AHP) to analyze the results from the negotiation mechanism. In this study, AHP is implied in choosing the suppliers of clothing process and consequently form an integrated network among the suppliers, the retailer, and the logistic provider.

This study applies negotiation mechanism and AHP to integrate buyer-driven supply chain in apparel industry. And it also provides a way for firms to improve product performance through short lead time, increased flexibility, and closer fit to market needs.

4

Conclusion

This research present two parts of different types supply chains, which are producer-driven and buyer-driven chain, applied in different industries. The most differences between these two types are: producer-driven supply chain is technology-intensive which needs a stable partner in long-term planning. So we use AHP to choose a preferred supplier firstly before negotiation. Nevertheless, buyer-driven supply chain is for labor-intensive which deals with dynamic changing in the apparel markets. In Chapter 2, supplier selection and evaluation is very important to the success of a manufacturing firm. Thus, the objective of this study is to develop an integrated analytic hierarchy process with negotiation mechanism which will help to solve the supplier selection problems to obtain the most beneficial offers for the buyer by creating strong competition between suppliers and providing a vehicle for negotiating with them. In Chapter 3, Retailers face many challenges: time-to-market reductions are necessary due to shorter and shorter product life cycles, greater product variety causing more fluctuation in demand calls for high responsiveness in supply chains. This chapter focus on how the third logistic provider organizes their supply chains in light of how they choose to compete in consumer markets. Therefore, we firstly use negotiation mechanism to get some potential suppliers with alternatives to be chosen from the retailer, and then use AHP to form an effective integrated network according to the fast-moving market. Consequently, these two chapters both explain how to negotiate between buyer and sellers and form an integrated supply chain to achieve win-win situation for all members in supply chain.

References

1. Bailey, J., & Bakos, Y. (1997). An exploratory study of the emerging role of electronic intermediaries, *International Journal of Electronic Commerce*, 1(3).

2. Banuelas, R., & Antony, J. (2004). Modified Analytic Hierarchy Process to Incorporate Uncertainty and Managerial Aspects, *International journal of Production Research*, 42(18), pp. 3851-3872.

3. Barborosoglu, G. & Yazgac, T. (1997). An application of the analytic hierarchy process to the supplier selection problem, *Production and Inventory Management Journal*, pp. 14-21. First quarter.

4. Bertsekas, D. P. (1995). Dynamic programming and optimal control. Athena Scientific, Belmont, MA.

5. Bhutta, K. S., & Huq, F. (2002), Supplier selection problem: a comparison of the total cost of ownership and analytic hierarchy process approaches, *Supply Chain Management: An International Journal*, 7(3), pp. 126-135.

6. Bitran, G. R., Gurumurthi, S., & Sam, S. L. (2006). Emerging Trends in Supply Chain Governance, Working Report 2006. Sloan School of Management, MIT, Cambridge, MA.

7. Braglia, M. & Petroni, A. (2000). A quality assurance-oriented methodology for handling tradeoffs in supplier selection, *International Journal of Physical Distribution & Logistics Management*, 30(2), pp. 96-111.

8. Brägger, M. (2004). Supply Chain Management and Collaboration in

the Apparel Sector – Learning from the Best? *International Commerce Review*. Europe.

9.   Brannon, E. L. (2000). Fashion Forecasting. New York. Fairchild.

10.   Buyukozkan, G., & Feyzioglu, O. (2004). A New Approach Based on Soft Computing to Accelerate the Selection of New Product Ideas, *Computers in Industry*, 54, pp. 151-167.

11.   Castro-Schez1, J. J., Jennings, N. R., Luo, X., & Shadbolt, N. R. (2004). Acquiring domain knowledge for negotiating agents: a case of study, *International Journal of Human-Computer Studies*, 61, pp. 3-31.

12.   Chen, Y.M. & Huang, P. N.(2009), Agent-based bilateral multi-issue negotiation scheme for e-market transactions, Applied *Soft Computing*, 9(3), pp. 1057-1067.

13.   Chen, Y. M., Goan, M. J., & Huang, P. N.,(2011), Selection process in logistics outsourcing – a view from third party logistics provider," *Production Planning & Control The Management of Operations*, 22 (3) pp. 308 – 324.

14.   Cyert, R. M., & DeGroot, M. H. (1987). Bayesian analysis and uncertainty in economic theory. Rowman & Littlefield, New York.

15.   Dickson, G. (1966). An analysis of vendor selection systems and decisions, *Journal of Purchasing*, 2(1), pp. 5- 17.

16.   Dubois, D., & Prade, H. (1980). Fuzzy Sets and Systems, Academic Press, New York.

17.   Dujmovic, J. J. (1975). Extended continuous logic and the theory of complex criteria. Series on Mathematics and Physic, 537, pp. 197-216.

18.   Gereffi, G. (2003). The Global Apparel Value Chain: What Prospects for Upgrading by Developing Countries. Vienna, Austria.

19.   Gereffi, G. (2001). Beyond the Producer-driven/Buyer-driven Dichotomy. The Evolution of Global Value Chains in the Internet Era, *IDS Bulletin*, 32(3), pp. 30-40.

20.   Gunasekaran, A., & Ngai, E. W. T. (2005). Build-to-order supply chain management: a literature review and framework for development, *Journal of Operations Management*, 23, pp. 423-451.

21.   He, M. (2004). Designing bidding strategies for autonomous trading agents. Ph.D. lecture note. UK: University of Southampton.

22.   Jennings, N. R., Faratin, P., Norman, T. J., O'Brien, P., Odgers, B., & Alty, J. L. (2000). Implementing a business process management system using ADEPT: A real-world case study, *International Journal of Applied Artificial Intelligence*, 14(5), pp. 421-465.

23.   Jiang, K., & Wicks, E.M. (1999). Integrated investment justification approach for cellular manufacturing systems using activity-based costing and the analytic hierarchy process, *Journal of Engineering Valuation and Cost Analysis*, 2 (4), pp. 271–284.

24.   Kim, J. S. (2003). Negotiation support in electronic commerce using fuzzy membership functions and AHP, *Proceedings of the 6th Pacific Rim International Workshop on Multi-Agents*, pp. 93-104. Seoul, Korea.

25.   Liu, J., Ding, F. Y., & Lall, V. (2000). Using data envelopment analysis to compare suppliers for supplier selection and performance improvement, *Supply Chain Management: An International Journal*, 5(3), pp. 143-150.

26.   Maes, P., Guttman, R. H., & Moukas, A. G. (1999). Agents that buy and sell. Communications of the ACM, 42(3), pp. 81-91.

27.   Mandal, A., & Deshmukh S. G. (1994). Vendor selection using interpretive structural modeling, *International Journal of Operations & Production Management*, 14(6), pp. 52-59.

28.   Masella, C. & Rangone, A. (2000). A contingent approach to the design of vendor selection systems for different types of co-operative customer/supplier relationship, *International Journal of Operations & Production Management*, 20(1), pp. 70-84.

29.   Muralisharan, C., Anantharaman, N., & Deshmukh, S. G. (2002). A multi-criteria group decisionmaking model for supplier rating, *The Journal of Supply Chain Management*, pp. 22-33. Fall.

30.   Narasimhan, R., Talluri S., & Mendez D. (2001). Supplier evaluation and rationalization via data envelopment analysis: An empirical examination, *The Journal of Supply Chain Management*, pp. 28-35. Summer.

31. Oliveira, R. C., & Lourenço, J. C. (2002). A multicriteria model for assigning new orders to service suppliers, *European Journal of Operational Research*, 139, pp. 390-399.

32. Pruitt, D. G. (1981). Negotiation Behavior. Academic Press.

33. Rahwan, I., Kowalczyk, R., & Pham, H. H. (2002). Intelligent agents for automated one-to-many e-commerce negotiation, *Proceedings of the twenty-fifth Australasian conference on Computer science*, pp. 197-204. Australia.

34. Raiffa, H. (1982). The art and science of negotiation. Cambridge, USA: Harvard University Press.

35. Rosenschein, J. S., & Zlotkin, G. (1994). Rules of Encounter. MIT Press.

36. SCC, (1999). Overview of the SCOR Model V2.0, Supply Chain Council, Inc., http://www.supply chain.org.

37. Selim, Z., Mehmet, S., & Mehves, T., Fuzzy Analytic Hierarchy Based Approach For Supplier Selection.

38. Sierra, C., Faratin, P., & Jennings, N. R. (2000). Deliberative automated negotiators using fuzzy similarities, *Proceedings of EUSFLAT*, pp. 155-158.

39. Steel, P. T., & Beasor (1999). Business negotiation: A practical workbook, Gower Publishing Limited.

40. Su, Y. W., Huang, C., Hammer, J., Huang, Y., Li, H., Wang, L., Liu, Y., Pluempitiwiriyawej, C., Lee, M., & Lam, H. (2001). An internet-based negotiation server for e-commerce. The VLDB Journal, 10, pp. 72-90.

41. Subramani, M., & Walden, E. (2000). Economic returns to firms from business-to-business electronic commerce initiatives: an empirical examination, *In: Proceedings of the twenty first international conference on information systems*, pp. 229-241.

42. Tam, M. C. Y. & Tummala, V. M. R. (2001). An application of the AHP in vendor selection of a telecommunication system, *Omega*, 29, pp. 171-182.

43. Vokurka, J. R., Choobineh, J., & Vadi, L. (1996). A prototype expert

system for the evaluation and selection of potential suppliers, *International Journal of Operations & Production Management*, 16(12), pp. 106-127.

44.   Wang, G., Huang, S. H., & Dismukes, J. P. (2004). Product-driven Supply Chain Selection using Integrated Multi-criteria Decision-making Methodology, *International journal of Production Economics*, 91, pp. 1-15.

45.   Wong, W. Y., Zhang, D. M., & Kara-Ali, M. (2000). Negotiating with experience. In: KBEM-2001. Austin, TX.

46.   Xudong, L., Nicholas, R. J., & Nigel, S. (2003). Acquiring Tradeoff Preferences for Automated Negotiations: A Case Study. Southampton, UK.

47.   Yan, H., Yu Z., Cheng, & T. C. E. (2003). A Strategic model for supply chain design with logical constraints: formulation and solution, *Computers & Operations Research*, pp. 1-21. September.

48.   Zeng, D., & Sycara, K. (1998). Bayesian learning in negotiation, *International Journal of Human Computer Studies*, 48, pp. 125-141.